Living Expectantly

Extraordinary Living In an Ordinary World

ELAINE KEITH

Printed in the United States of America
©2014 Elaine Keith
All rights reserved

Library of Congress Cataloging-in-Publication Data
ISBN: 9781609200992

API
Ajoyin Publishing, Inc.
P.O. 342
Three Rivers, MI 49093
www.ajoyin.com

No part of this book may be reproduced or transmitted in any form or by any means, electronic or mechanical—including photocopying, recording, or by any information storage and retrieval system—without permission in writing from the publisher, except as provided by United States of America copyright law.

Please direct your inquiries to admin@ajoyin.com

Book design by:
Kyle Keith and Michael Regina.
To contact author: cflslc@sbcglobal.net

Unless otherwise noted, all Scripture quotations are from the Holy Bible, New American Standard Version. Other versions abbreviated as follows:
LB (Living Bible)
AMP (The Amplified Version)
NLT (New Living Translation)
JBP (J.B.Phillips)
The Message

Some names have been changed

To Our Grandchildren

"God, You have taught me everything I know. Now I'm telling my grandchildren Your wonders; and I will keep on until I am old and gray." PSALM 71:17-18
THE MESSAGE

Unless the fires of Christianity continue to burn then we could be just one generation away from becoming extinct. This book is dedicated to you, these are our stories of all God has done. He is the God of limitless resources and He wants to make Himself real to each of you. As your grandparents we have set the ceiling for our faith and our ceiling can become your floor. May you rise higher than we ever have and may you change your corner of the world. We declare and decree that our grandchildren and their children shall be mighty upon this earth. JOB 22:28 AND PSALM 112:2

Mimi and Gramps

Kristina Kay	Stacey Leigh
Jamie Leigh (who is waiting in heaven)	Karolyn Elaine
	Hannah Kathryn
Nathan Keith	Judah Reeves
Sara Elizabeth	Laura Elaine
Katy Ann	Joshua Kyle
Kortney Jordan	James Turner
Stephanie Anne	Andrew Kelly

[In the] Book of Ecclesiastes, God is saying . . . Write a good story, take somebody with you and let me help.

Donald Miller, *A Million Miles in a Thousand Years*

This book will fill you with hope and awe and wonder of God once again. As you see Him work in the trials, challenges, and everyday life, and make what **seems** impossible into the possible by turning those things into triumphs and victories!

Elaine captures your heart with the gift of storytelling as she brings life through truth, laughter, and tears. Her wonderful southern accent makes me want to listen to everything she writes as I can hear her voice even while I read. For those of you who don't know her, she has a gift of hospitality to go along with it. When you are with her, you feel truly cared for and loved. Her mother would be so proud.

I have co-labored together with Elaine for several years and I have enjoyed her sense of humor immensely. She brings peace and strength into situations
which enables those around her to feel loved; she has a heart full of passion for people.

With her wonderful command of the Scriptures and teaching gift, God has used her to help others all over the world obtain freedom in their own lives. Elaine has made a mark in history and in the lives of many. "Well done, good and faithful servant! BUT you aren't done yet"

Thank you, Elaine, for being real and standing no matter what!

>Cheryl Kirkham
>Zion Christian Fellowship, Powell, Ohio
>Transformation Center Director
>Sozo Healing Ministry

Contents

The Beginning of the End 1
Let Go of the Old and Embrace the New 5
Forgiveness Is Not an Option 15
What about Our Children? 25
Messy In the Middle 33
Learning to Lean On Him 49
The Storm 59
The Storm Continues 69
The Wilderness 83
Move That Mountain of Fear 97
The Honeymoon Is Over 107
The Miracle of the Green Dress 121
No Longer Will We Eat Manna 129
Seattle, Here We Come 147
It's Off to Work I Go 155
My Heart Has Been Enlarged for the Nations 165
World, Here We Come 175
Leaving My Thumbprint on the Nations 187
Coming Out of Hiding 199
Eating at the King's Table 219
One More Thing 229

Epilogue 231

INTRODUCTION

"Jesus also did many other things. If they were all written down, I suppose the whole world could not contain the books that would be written." John 21:25 (NLT)

Even though our story was not recorded in this BOOK, it is a story than needs to be told because Jesus is the One that caused it to come about. Notice the tree on the cover of this book? If this tree could talk it would have many interesting stories to share. What you might not have noticed, the tree is damaged. You see, it was struck by lightening and not only that, but it had weathered many storms. This tree is symbolic of what our life was at one time.

Shortly after we moved into this present home lightening struck this ole' oak. It burned and burned and aroused all the neighbors and they came running to see what was causing such a terrible smell and loud sound.. We called the specialist out, an arborist. He took one look at this tree that had become so damaged and told us we needed to take the tree down. Not only could it become diseased, but should that happen then the trees around this tree could become affected. It was sad!

Yes, this seemed so much like what our life had once been. Every counselor that we sought seemed to think that our marriage was diseased and there was no hope. Divorce was the only answer. Resentment and anger were eating away at the heart of our lives and those around us. Bitterness had taken deep root. Our children were definitely being negatively affected. We were so damaged! Our scars were ugly! Was there any hope for our family? Should we be "taken down?"

We loved that ole' oak so we decided to take a chance on that tree. With care and tenderness the tree began to heal and though it has remained scarred, it provides the most wonderful shade on a hot summer day. Jesus took a chance on us and with His healing balm we too have survived. We have faced many storms, some more severe than others, and though you might still see some scars, in spite of all this He has used us to provide "shade" for others. This is our story and our journey proving the faithfulness of God.

The Beginning of the End

We had been shut in the house for days due to the snow. We were all going stir crazy! Unfortunately, Christmas had not been the wonderful, peaceful, and loving holiday the movies depict. I could feel the pressure mounting and I wasn't sure I could hold in my anger any longer. Something had to give between Bill and myself or we would have to bring this marriage to an end!

When did it first begin to go sour? Who can say? Doesn't an apple begin to deteriorate after it has become bruised? But who knows how long it has been in that condition before one notices the eating away of the fruit. That was our marriage! Bruises, hurts, unexpressed feelings too deep to even try and identify. It was like a ball of twine. Where would we start trying to unravel and untangle this huge quagmire of differences?

My parents were visiting and they could feel the tension, but as always they were hoping "this too would pass." During the night Bill and I had gotten in a terrible argument and gone downstairs hoping no one would hear us hash it out. I don't remember what this particular argument was about, but the stress of the moment was accelerating and as Bill had a habit of doing, he turned his back on me and walked away.

For whatever reason I could not take this any longer, the rejection, the passivity, the seemingly not caring. Why wouldn't he talk to me? Without too much thought I picked up a pair of scissors and threw them. This kind of action always seemed to get his attention. And that night it certainly did! Without any particular aim I had thrown the scissors directly into an antique china cabinet that had been in his family for a number of years. The beveled glass shattered and not only did it gain Bill's attention, the household was awakened!

Both my parents came running down the stairs and by now Bill and I were having heated words! He was furious. I had broken the original glass on this beautiful antique piece of furniture. Isn't it strange that a piece of furniture seemed more important to him than our marriage that was falling apart slowly but surely? Now our parents and children were part of this uninvited audience. My mother screamed out, "This can't go on! Look what you are doing to your children. You must get a divorce!"

Coming from my mother those were very sobering words as my mother hated divorce. She had seen the devastation of divorce when my only brother had gotten a divorce, eventually gaining custody of his young son and then bringing him back for my mother to virtually raise for almost 6 years. Yes, she hated divorce and yet she is saying we must get one!

After all these years of fighting and arguing we still loved one another, we just didn't know how to live in harmony with one another. We had brought a lot of baggage into our marriage, things we had never dealt with.

Our marriage had started out for all the wrong reasons and now years later the attractions that drew us together could no longer keep us together. What were we to do? Were we just destined to become another statistic of a broken home? Another marriage that didn't quite work out due to irreconcilable differences?

No chance of reconciliation? What about our children? Would they be divided between their parents? Would they have to make choices of who they would live with? Deep down we did not want to do that to them, but what could we do? Was there any hope?

Let Go of the Old and Embrace the New

Several months passed and things were better between us, but certainly nothing had been resolved. As with every other problem, we just swept this under the carpet and acted like all was well. Frankly, I wasn't sure how much longer we could keep walking on this "carpet" as the lumps were taking over.

We continued to attend church regularly. On Sunday mornings we put on our Sunday faces just like we put on our Sunday clothes. To the outside world we looked like the ideal family, but inwardly it was becoming harder and harder to keep up the façade.

People were getting excited about the upcoming meetings that many in our church had signed up to attend. Personally I was grumbling. I thought it was quite un-Christian to be required to pay to attend classes in order to learn how to share our faith. In fact, I had almost talked myself out of going, but since I had already signed up and paid the registration fee, I decided to attend the first meeting, mainly out of pride. I didn't want my church friends to think I didn't want to attend this meeting. So like I seemed to live my life, I would do what was necessary to keep face.

The evening of the first meeting I had arranged for friends to pick me up. Bill was out of town and would not be able to attend any of the meetings unless he rearranged his schedule, but he had not signed up for the meetings at this point. Again, I was complaining in my heart and wondering what the world was coming to when someone had to pay to learn more about God.

I dressed very carefully as I always tried to do. Every hair was in place, my makeup perfectly applied, and I had chosen one of my favorite dresses to wear that morning. It was bright red, hopefully it would lift my negative disposition although I seriously doubted it would help. Why didn't I just donate the money and not commit to attend the meetings? I was becoming quite put out with myself for making such a foolish decision to attend something in which I was not the least bit interested.

Driving into the parking lot, we had a hard time finding a place to park. It was almost full and this was a large parking area and building. We all went inside, found seats where we could sit together, and waited for the meeting to begin. I was already bored and the meeting had not even started.

We gathered in a large auditorium, men and women together, although I found out we would eventually divide and the women would go into another area later in the evening. Someone came to the podium and announced the guest speaker and then opened with prayer. This nice looking fellow approached the podium and began sharing a little about himself. It seems he had been a very successful businessman; in fact he was a millionaire. I was thinking in my heart, "Why would someone like him want to be at one of these boring meetings?"

He shared how he felt led to give up his prosperous business and go into full time service for the Lord. I thought to myself, "this guy must have been nuts and is probably a religious fanatic." But, for whatever reason, he had my attention. There was something about the way he spoke, the things he said, that made me sit up and listen attentively. The way he talked you would have thought he knew Jesus Christ personally. Never before had I heard someone talk about God in such an intimate and appealing way. I was intrigued.

In the course of his sharing he began to talk about sin. By now I was becoming quite uncomfortable and wishing I had sat on the aisle seat, then I would have un-

> **Never before had I heard someone talk about God in such an intimate and appealing way. I was intrigued.**

obtrusively gotten up and left the auditorium. But keep in mind, I am sitting with all the people I attend church with. As always I had to keep face! Why had I come to this meeting? I knew I should have stayed home. This was not for me, but I could not get up without someone noticing.

I began to do a checklist in my mind to see if I had broken any of the Ten Commandments. After all he was talking about sin. Well, let me see, oh sure as a teenager

I probably had not honored my parents especially when I would smart talk my mother. But wasn't this typical of any teenager? I lied, but only occasionally.

I didn't have any other gods. Look, I was a Christian. I went to church regularly, threw a few dollars in the offering occasionally. I didn't worship Buddha or any of those things. Actually, I felt I was a pretty good person, especially when I compared myself to some of those hypocrites in our church. I had never committed adultery although at times I had thought about it; but I never followed through and of course I had never murdered anyone, although I had thought about that when I would get so angry at my husband! Besides, if other women had put up with some of the things I had put up with they might have felt the same way. Yes, the more I compared myself with others the better I was feeling about myself.

But suddenly I heard this man talking about jealousy, envy, pride, fear, anger, and hatred. Now it seemed like he was talking directly to me. Did he know me? Had some of the people from the church come by and heard me screaming at Bill and the children and told him to be sure and address these things? It was strange. He seemed to know so much about me.

In the meantime the ushers had passed out sheets of paper and now this man was telling us to write down all the things we could identify with. I was becoming very uncomfortable and angry. What right did this perfect stranger have to address these things? This was a private matter. Oh, if only I could have gotten up I would have. How could I write down these things with people from my church sitting on either side of me. What if they could read my list?

I still don't know why I did what he suggested, but I began to write very quickly trying to keep up with him. After all, practically everything he had mentioned I could identify with. Now he said, "At the top of your paper write down this scripture, I John 1:9" Then he read this scripture aloud. *"If we confess our sins, He is faithful and righteous to forgive us our sins and to cleanse us from all unrighteousness."* He even emphasized the word "ALL."

Funny, I was beginning to feel lighter, not so heavy hearted. Maybe this meeting wouldn't be so bad after all. Then the man told us we could burn the paper, throw it away, whatever. We could get rid of it and I desperately wanted to, lest someone would see it. I was just thankful he didn't tell us to write our name on the paper and give it to an usher. Had he done that I would have pretended I was ill and left the room.

We broke for refreshments and I needed something. My mouth felt so dry. What was happening to me? The women were directed to another room and I found myself a seat in the back of the room. I couldn't believe how many women were in attendance and some of them so sharp looking. Many were dressed in the latest styles. I don't know why but I had expected rather dowdy looking women to attend something of this nature.

In the meantime the leader had come into the room and was standing behind the podium. She was so attractive. She introduced herself and I realized she was the wife of the man that had led the previous session. She was the wife of that millionaire. They had given all that up to "follow the Lord," whatever that meant. She and her husband looked like executives. Neither of them looked like people that would stand in a church pulpit and talk about God. All of this was very strange to me.

Well, she too talked like she knew Jesus Christ personally. What kind of people were they? Her part was to actually teach us to share our faith and she had a little booklet that she was using to train us. Remember, the purpose of this meeting was for us to learn how to share our faith. Earlier I had overheard someone say that in this booklet there was a prayer that many people had prayed and lives were being changed and transformed. I knew one thing, if I could get hold of that booklet I would pray that prayer and I was so desperate if I even had to steal the little booklet I would do that. My life was a mess and I needed something to change me!

The leader looked around the room as she told us she needed someone to play the part of the person she would be instructing how to share their faith. I deliberately looked down as I did not want to make eye contact with her. I was in the back of the room and I doubted if she could even see me. I would estimate there were at least 150 women in this room. Suddenly she said, "You in the red dress, come up." I looked around and she motioned to me and again said, "You in the red dress." By now I knew she meant me. I reluctantly rose from my seat and made my way to the front of the room. I was dreading this!

Now, she said, "I am going to go over this booklet with you. I will read and you just answer the questions as I ask them." She was demonstrating how we could do this with others. She said something about there being physical laws that govern the universe and also spiritual laws. This was something I had never heard before. I wasn't quite sure what she meant, but she had my attention. I was listening very intently.

She proceeded to read from the booklet. "Law one, God loves you and has a wonderful plan for your life." At that moment I began to shake my head. I wasn't sure I had heard her correctly. Did she say, "God loved me and had a wonderful plan for my life?" I was pondering that statement. Was that true? Could I dare believe that this God that had created me had a purpose for my life? And to think, this God, the God of the universe, creator of all things and all people, loved me. It was almost too much for my mind to comprehend. In all my years I had <u>never</u> heard anyone say that God loved me! The thought was staggering!

As a child I distinctly remember hearing over and over again, "If you aren't good, God will not love you." Growing up I was quite headstrong and rebellious, very moody, and with a horrible temper. I was told daily how bad I was and then was compared to a family member that everyone knew was bad. That tape played in my mind daily. "You are BAD! You are just like so and so!" I knew I could never meet God's standard, whatever that might be, so I gave up on God very early in my life. I believed He did not and could not love me. But I was standing there listening to that stranger tell me that God loves me. It was almost too much. Why, I don't know, but I believed everything this woman was sharing with me. I wanted to cry! I had never in all my life heard such Good News!

My mind was racing. I was trying to listen to everything she was saying, but the words she had spoken were like a delicious meal and I wanted to savor every minute and not rush through this. I knew I should answer her questions, but my heart was soaking up these words of hope. I felt like a dry desert that suddenly was being rained on and I dare not let go in the event if would stop.

All these years I had run from Him! My mother often told me that, even as a little girl, when I would do something wrong I would immediately say, "And I don't love God and I don't love Jesus!" If He wasn't going to love me, then I would not give Him the satisfaction of thinking I loved Him. I had always believed there was a God. I never doubted His existence, but I did not know Him. I only knew of Him. Do you see the difference?

I never doubted He created me, but to believe He had a purpose for me? That was hard to imagine. Often I would think about Him being in heaven looking down on me and just waiting for a chance to zap me each and every time I messed up. I felt the day He created me He

Was that true? Could I dare believe that this God that had created me had a purpose for my life?

---

must have dumped me on this earth and said something like this. "OK, Kid, here you are. Don't call Me. I'll call you if need be." I know that sounds ridiculous, but seriously, that was my interpretation of what I thought God was like.

Standing here with the leader of this group I felt like

scales were falling from my eyes, the weights were being lifted off of me. I thought of the time I had taken all those pills wanting to end my life because I felt my life was such a mistake and so hopeless. Why live I would ask myself? I was miserable and I seemed to make life miserable for those around me. But this woman was telling me, "God loves you. He has a plan for your life." Somewhere I heard someone speaking to me and realized the leader was asking me a question. "How did I know this was true?" And I quickly answered and said, "Because I feel like it!" She immediately corrected me and said, "Oh no, you can't base it on feelings. You must base it on what God's Word says." Of course at that time I had no idea what the Word said, I only knew something was different. I was now seeing life from a different perspective. I was loved, I had purpose and I wanted to live!

"Behold, the former things have come to pass, Now I declare new things; Before they spring forth I proclaim them to you." ISAIAH 42:9

That was a defining moment. Something significantly changed in my heart during those meetings. God met me right where I was. I was reminded of that night when Bill and I had gotten into such an ugly battle and my mother said we needed to get a divorce. After we had gone to bed that night I prayed a desperate prayer, "O Lord, help, help me, help us!" I believe God heard my prayer and although it had been awhile since I had cried out for help, when I prayed the prayer that was in the little booklet at that meeting—the prayer I had heard others say was changing lives—that was the turning point not only for me, but for our marriage and our family, the family everyone had given up on, That is, everyone but Almighty God. He heard and He sent help! His eye is on the sparrow and His eye was on us.

As strange as this may sound, this is where my story of purpose began. Suddenly I knew I was born for a reason. I was not an accident as I had been told. I had been planned by Almighty God. I can remember as a young girl looking in the mirror and asking myself, "Who am I? Why am I here?" Now I knew. I had met my Creator!

Forgiveness Is Not an Option

It was a new beginning. I could hardly wait to come back for the rest of the meetings and I wanted my husband to come and be touched just as I had been. Bill came home sooner than expected and I invited him to attend the evening meeting with me. He later said when he walked in the house that evening he knew in his heart something had happened to me. It was obvious. I had been with Jesus.

I did not know at the time that Bill had made a commitment to the Lord as a young teen when he attended a youth meeting. Unfortunately he was never encouraged in the things of the Lord and once he left home to attend college he walked away from the Lord. Bill went to the meeting with me and that evening he, too, made a commitment to follow the Lord. Now we were on the right track. I wish I could say, "Now we lived happily ever after," but that would be a lie. As I already mentioned, we each brought a lot of baggage into our marriage; we had buried so many hurts from our past, things we had never dealt with, things we had buried alive. In other words, when you don't resolve these things they will rise up at some point and come back to haunt you. That is burying them alive.

Now that we were getting right spiritually we knew we needed help. I would have to say that the majority, if not all, of our problems begin as a spiritual problem. I often would think, "If Bill would change, then we would have a better marriage." Unbeknownst to me, he was thinking the same thing, "If only Elaine would change." But the truth of the matter was, we both needed to change and the only way we could change was by hav-

> **I came into marriage with certain expectations about what I thought a husband should do or be and Bill had his own expectations about what he thought the wife's role in a marriage should be.**

ing a changed heart and only God can change a person from the inside out. Yes, we can change our behavior, but so often that change does not last for long. We were both disappointed in our marriage, it had not turned out the way we thought. I came into marriage with certain expectations about what I thought a husband should do or be and Bill had his own expectations about what he thought the wife's role in a marriage should be. We had never discussed any of these things with each other, we just assumed what we thought a marriage should be and what our mate would do. Today many marriages are on the rocks partly because the dream of what a marriage is going to be and the reality of what it really is are so different from each other. Disappointment often stems from unrealistic and unfulfilled expectations. Girls, let me give you a little bit of wisdom at this time. I spent a lot of time and effort trying to change my husband. I wanted him to conform to my idea of what I thought I needed in a husband. I have since learned, the only male you can change is the one in diapers. Give it up!

We knew we needed help and God led us to a wonderful counselor. He was very wise and gave us much sound advice. Of course, the first thing addressed was forgiving one another. Bill was always the first to ask for forgiveness when we would argue, but for the most part it was never as a result of repentance, but only wanting to clear the air. There is a difference in being a peacekeeper and a peacemaker. A peacekeeper will do anything to keep peace, even take the blame just so they can move on. A peacemaker will do what is necessary in order to bring peace and many times that can be like walking into a war zone.

But when we are willing to work on it, talk about the issues and decide we are not afraid of conflict resolution, then we can move past the problem and come into a much healthier place and communicate with each other the way God wants. Often we play the blame game, bring up the past, and don't take responsibility for what we have done. When we blame the other party, they can become defensive. We must learn to express how we are feeling or what we think. When the counselor talked to us about forgiving one another, it was very hard for me. Bill had been unfaithful in our marriage and I had held onto this. Though I had said I forgave him, I really had not. To tell you the truth I didn't even know how to forgive and let go, the pain was so deep. By holding on and not forgiving, it was like a weapon for me to use against him. You women probably know what I mean, right?!? I could remind him of his past and it gave me some leverage in the situation. Knowing what I know today I would call that what it really is: REVENGE!!

Revenge is wanting to punish the other person and that was what I was wanting to do. By holding onto my pain I felt I was punishing him, but in reality I was being controlled by my own actions. So many times I would rage. I have since learned when a person rages it is either because they don't have the courage or the ability to express what they are truly feeling. At that time in my life I believed the only way a person would listen to me was when I screamed and hollered. It got their attention. I had never learned how to express the deep feelings within my heart. I did not know myself. I did not have a clue how to speak out of my heart. I couldn't even identify my feelings. I only knew I was angry!

Anger is actually a secondary emotion. We move into anger because we are denying the emotion that triggered the anger. For instance; sometimes it is hard to admit you are fearful or you are feeling rejected, so we bypass that first emotion and move into the secondary emotion—anger.

Now please understand what I am about to say. I personally feel sexual immorality is one of the worst things a couple can commit within a marriage, but I also understand how destructive and damaging bitterness, resentment, anger, and rage can be to a relationship. These things can be like a poison that eats away and erodes the foundation and eventually there is nothing left on which to build. So we need to make sure that we deal with these things and not allow the enemy to have a foothold in our life.

Being honest with God and ourselves is the only way to get rid of these things. We must allow God to shine His light into the deep recesses of our heart, those hidden places if need be, and agree with Him when He shows us these things that are not of Him. It's His kindness that shows us the negative things filed away in our heart. Yes, Bill had been unfaithful and he had failed, but I too had failed. But with Christ on our side we were learning even these things were redeemable. Though we were moving forward we still had a lot to learn as a couple.

When this counselor talked to me about forgiving Bill, I was not sure I could. The wound was still bleeding or so it seemed. He asked me, "Are you willing to forgive him?" I told him I knew it was the right thing to forgive but I didn't know if I could. I knew I needed to let go of the past, but how? He then said to me, "Are you willing for God to help you be willing?" That seemed like something I could agree with. He prayed with me and God began a work in my heart to be willing to forgive Bill.

You see, God works with us where we are. He knew my deep hurt and pain. There are places in our heart that only God can touch. By being willing for God to help me, I finally came to the place of letting go. And now I

God works with us where we are.
---

needed to ask Bill to forgive me as I had failed him in many ways. As I look back on this I can see that it wasn't just what Bill had done, but I had been so rejected by others throughout my life and what Bill did only triggered those things already hidden deep within my subconscious. God was exposing some deep roots within my own heart and in His timing He would help me deal with those things.

Forgiveness doesn't mean we overlook the offense; that would not be honest and it can also be damaging. To deny you have been hurt or wronged will not bring healing. That is like putting a band-aid on the injury, but not looking at the cause of the injury. As painful as it might be, the only way to get free is to face it honestly, see it for what it is, experience the emotion, the pain, and ask God to help you and He will. People that are shame-based are experts at stuffing their emotions. They become quite skilled in "talking words," but not "feeling words." That defined where I had been most of my life. I talked a lot, but totally bypassed my feelings and as a result I was full of rage.

Let me give you an example of what I mean by "talking words and feeling words." I could talk and tell you how angry I was with something my husband may have done. I might have said something like this, "Yeah, I think he was a jerk for doing that and it made me furious." I would describe that as "talking words." But it would not touch the deep hurt, the wound. Now, had I been able to express my emotions at that time, I would have said something like this, "I felt totally betrayed. I felt he no longer loved me, or desired me. I was afraid. I felt I had failed as a wife, a woman." That is what I call "feeling words." Once I was able to look at and express my emotions, then the anger could be dispelled.

Forgiveness is not for the perpetrator, it is for yourself; to choose to forgive yourself frees you! When we hold on to the offense then we become the victim. True forgiveness gives us back our life. Forgiveness is not passivity, it is just the opposite. It is POWER! Walter Wangerin said, *"True forgiveness is a divine absurdity."* Yes, in the natural it does not make sense to forgive if you have been wronged, but it works and besides that, you are being obedient to what Scripture tells us in Matthew 18.

The beautiful thing I have learned about God is that in His economy He does not waste anything . . . NOTHING!! It's like being in the recycling business. He takes the ugliest and most damaging thing and somehow turns it for good and makes something beautiful from it. Think about Isaiah 61:3, the divine exchange, *"Giving them a garland instead of ashes, the oil of gladness instead of mourning. The mantle of praise instead of a spirit of fainting."*

With God, from our greatest pain can come our greatest purpose and passion. From our misery can come our ministry. As God began to heal our marriage and we began to share all God had done, doors began to open for me to share all God was doing and was still doing in our life. Some women asked me to start a Bible study. Keep in mind, I was as "green as a gourd" as they would say in Texas. In other words I felt I knew nothing, but when we are willing to trust the Lord He equips us for the occasion.

Before we go any further you might notice from time to time I revert to my Texas colloquialism even in writing. Hey, you might even hear my twang . . . now that would be a miracle! As I try to explain to people when they don't understand me . . . Texas is my first language and English is my second. So bear with me!

Once I had given my heart to the Lord I started attending a small Bible study and prayer group. I began to study the word of God. Actually, I was devouring it and loving it. I stepped out in faith and wrote up a little study for women, opened my home, and God brought women from all around to attend this group. We had three women that drove over one hundred miles each week in order to attend this study. They were hungry and I was amazed at all God was doing.

I felt the Lord told me to call this study, "God's Ideal Woman." I wasn't sure I liked that title, but eventually He told me His ideal woman was one that trusted Him no matter what. In the beginning, I taught this class for ten weeks but later condensed it to an eight week class. It was a wonderful time of fellowship and learning for all of us. As I taught, God was also teaching me. Teaching should always be for the teacher as well as the student.

As I taught in my home, word began to spread and now churches were inviting me to come and speak. Before I knew it I was teaching several classes a week. Then doors began to open for me to come and share my testimony of how God was healing our marriage and eventually Bill and I both were being asked to share as a couple. Although we still had such a long way to go, it was nothing short of a miracle of what God had done and was continuing to do. The women attending the classes began to complain that their husbands needed to learn these principles of marriage, so Bill and I opened our home and held classes in our home. Eventually the need became greater and we outgrew our home and started teaching in churches. At some point we started a non-profit ministry and called it "God's Ideal Family." We stood in awe as we saw how God was using us to help other couples and families.

Was it because we were so special or because we now had our act together that God was using us? No, not at all! II Corinthians 4:7 tell us, *"We have this treasure in earthen vessels., so that the surpassing greatness of the power will be of God and not from ourselves."* Bill and I were so aware of how imperfect we still were, we were nothing more than a clay pot but we could carry His Presence with us to a lost and dying world. And we made ourselves available for Him to use us however He chose. He was giving us a message to couples and families.

Let me share a few tips that might enhance your communication skills. Some people are naturally better communicators than others, but it is an art, something that one can learn and one in which we can become more skilled. I call this the ABC's of communicating or I should say, "some of the ABC's."

Always treat the other person with respect.

Be a listener, not always a talker.

Confront the problem, not the person.

Define the conflict (you might think it is one thing and they think something else).

Explain how you see the problem.

Focus on the present problem, don't bring up the past.

Give your full attention to the one talking without interrupting.

Honestly express your heart *without* blaming the other person.

Instant defensiveness can arise from saying something like this, "You always, or you never."

Judgments should be left up to God.

Keep short accounts.

Love covers a multitude of sin.

What about Our Children?

Things in our marriage definitely were better, although we still had a lot to learn. We were excited about everything God was doing with us as a couple. It truly was miraculous. One day we're ready for the divorce court and the next we're so happy to still be together. It had to have been obvious to our children that something was different, but I'm not sure they understood what had happened. I would suspect they were a little nervous wondering if another blow-up was just around the corner.

Now, you might find this hard to believe, but up until now I had never realized how much our fighting and arguing had damaged our children. I'm not trying to make excuses, but having grown up in an environment that was often like a war zone, this had become the "norm" for me. I must admit I always felt badly for our children hearing us and would usually make a point of trying to soothe them after the battles.

I knew nothing about the emotional damage that was taking place within their own little hearts. For so many years Bill and I would make threats of leaving one another and many times one of us would pack our bags and leave. I never had anyplace to go, but often I would pile the children and our belongings into the car and drive and drive for hours and then finally return home. At that time I was just in a mode of survival. Even today, so many years later, it is hard to visit those places of our past, but in doing so I am hoping to help you where you might be today and let you see there is hope.

I guess I would describe it as *the scales had come off my eyes!* Suddenly I became aware of the hurt, the pain, the fears, the rejection we had caused our children. Our children whom we loved so much and yet had damaged so badly. I can remember crying out to God, "What can we do to save our children?" To me it looked impossible and yet, I was learning with God all things are possible. Shortly after that while reading from the Bible I found a scripture in Joel 2:25 that spoke so loudly to my heart at that moment. This is just my own paraphrase, but it said, *I will restore unto you the years the locusts have eaten away.* This was a promise of restoration, and I was going to claim restoration for my children. Now, I know there are scholars that would refute this and perhaps say I took

To me it looked impossible and yet, I was learning with God all things are possible.

it out of context, that it was not written for me or whatever, but this is one of the ways that God has chosen to speak to me through the years. He will quicken His Word to my spirit and I will know that I know I can stand on that particular scripture. It is like a rhema word,,.alive in my spirit! And for you that don't know what a rhema word is, it is a word that God quickens to your spirit and you know that you know He is speaking to you.

There were four different types of locust that had been eating away at that tree; one would eat at the roots, another at the bark, another the foliage, and another at the fruit. The plan was to corrupt and eventually destroy that tree. But here is the good news—the tree was still standing. That was our children, our family. The locusts had tried to destroy us. They had eaten away at us in so many ways, but we were still standing. We were worth salvaging and that is what God sent His Son to do, *"heal the brokenhearted, set the captive free and send forth delivered those that were bruised, crushed, broken down by calamity . . . oppressed by superior force."* (LUKE 4:18 AMP.) I now had hope and I knew help was on its way! Another scripture also spoke life to my heart. It was found in the book of Isaiah, chapter 42:3. I love this scripture. *"A bruised reed He will not break, and a dimly burning wick He will not extinguish."* Isaiah was prophesying that when Christ the Messiah would come He would not discard those that were bruised and damaged. His ministry would be to restore them to what He intended for them from the beginning. The religious leaders in that day, the Pharisees, had nothing to do with those that had failed in life. In their mind these bruised people were of no use, just outcasts, if you will.

A reed was used to make musical instruments, but should they become bruised or broken it was no longer of any value and had to be cast aside for no longer could it be used to make music. But Isaiah was giving this analogy of the time when Jesus would come He would take those that were damaged and make them instruments of beauty that could play songs of His grace and majesty. This was our family, our children, and God was turning the tide of the enemy and in His timing, we would be those instruments to bring Him glory and grace. We would be trophies of His grace.

We have three children, two boys and one girl. Our daughter is the middle child. At this time our oldest son was almost fifteen, our daughter was thirteen and we were beginning to struggle through those teen age years. My mother would often refer to it as those "mean age years." I know that sounds funny, but I have since learned that we can bind our children, or anyone by the labels we put on them, the words that we speak over them that are negative. We are to bless with our mouth and not curse.

Words are images. Negative words can transform a person into a negative image. Words can become beliefs and direct our lives in a positive way or a negative way. Think about this, if someone says to you over and over "you are stupid, you will never amount to anything" it isn't long until you begin to believe that and act it out in your life. On the other hand, if someone tells you "You are wonderful. I believe you can do anything in life you set your mind to." Those words can propel you into a very bright future. I've heard it said, "Words can be like an atom bomb, handle them carefully." Don't look for the dirt, but dig for the gold! There is gold in each of us.

Bill was still traveling with his company and due to his large territory he was away most of the week and normally only home on week ends. We were beginning

Living Expectantly

to feel the tension this kind of situation can bring. Now that our relationship was changing and we were getting along much better we were wanting to be together and be partners in raising our family so we began to pray for wisdom as to what to do.

One weekend when Bill got home he shared some things with me that he felt God was speaking to him. He had been reading the Word and ran across the account of Moses and his failure to circumcise his sons. (EXODUS 4:24–26) Somehow in reading that, Bill felt he had been disobedient in not sharing with our children all that God was doing in our heart. We decided that we needed to give our children the opportunity to pray and ask Jesus to come into their heart. The two younger children were very open and eager to do this. Kelly was not quite ready to make that decision and that was okay. We wanted this to be Holy Spirit led and not our own doing.

Yes, we were a little disappointed, but we also felt it was wisdom to not try and force Jesus on him. What was happening in our home was huge, an enormous change

> **I now know it is better to talk more to God about your children, your spouse, or whoever, and talk less to the person about God.**

in our relationship, and sometimes it takes awhile for everyone to come on board. I now know it is better to talk more to God about your children, your spouse, or whoever, and talk less to the person about God. How did I come about this conclusion? The hard way! I tried to force feed things not only to my children and my husband but to others too. One day I felt the Lord spoke to my heart and said, "Elaine, I am Bill's Holy Spirit. You can step back!" I had lots of zeal in those early days and very little wisdom. I have learned some things can only be accomplished by praying them through.

One morning during my devotion time I came across a scripture that really caught my attention. *"Believe in the Lord Jesus, and you will be saved, you and your household."* ACTS 16:31. I continued to read this over and over several times. Was this a promise for my family? I felt God told me I could believe for my household. If this was true—and I knew it was—then that meant I could pray and have the assurance that Kelly would one day surrender to the Lord. Early in my walk I began to "pray read" the scriptures. In other words, when I found a promise about something or someone that I was praying about, I would insert their names in that particular scripture. I don't remember that anyone had taught me to do that, I just started doing it and now all these years later I see how effective it is. Here's an example . . . *"God, You said, if I would believe on the Lord Jesus Christ I would be saved. I have done that and then You said, 'you and your household.' So, Lord, I bring Kelly to your throne and I thank you that salvation is coming to him. Amen!"*

I also love this scripture found in I John 5:14–15 *"This is the confidence that we have before Him, that if we ask anything according to His will, He hears us. And if we know that He hears us in whatever we ask, we <u>know</u> that we have the requests which we have asked from Him."*

Now that does not mean they automatically will come to the Lord, but in God's timing we can trust it will happen. I encourage you to start standing in the gap for your family members, declaring what God's Word says and watch what God will do! With this promise under our belt we began to pray more fervently for our eldest son to also surrender to Jesus. I don't recall how long it was before Kelly made that decision, but eventually he did and of course we all rejoiced at that time. I will say at some point all three of our children walked away from the things we had taught them and our hearts were sad, but again we continued to stand in the gap, declare the promises of God, and now as I write this I can report that all three of our children love and serve the Lord and their spouses are also believers. God is faithful! **Learn to live expectantly!** Stand on His promises and watch how God fulfills His Word! As of this very moment, start acting like the Word of God is true. I promise you, it is! I know this from experience!

I believe so many people live their life without the power of God being manifest in their life. Have you discovered the power of prayer? Prayer is a supernatural weapon when used in the authority that God has bestowed on us as believers in Him. When we "pray read" the scriptures we are praying the Word of God. These are His words, His promises to us, His children. In II Corinthians 1:19–20 in the Living Bible I love what He says. The second part of verse 19 reads; *"He isn't one to say 'yes' when He really means 'no.' He always does exactly what He says. He carries out and fulfills <u>all of God's promises</u> no matter how many of them they are."*

God is looking for a people who will dare to prove the greatness of their God by praying bold prayers and not limiting God in any way. Learn to expect the unexpected. *LIVE EXPECTANTLY!* Living in expectancy of what God can do and Who God is can take us into levels we would have never thought could happen.

"Now to Him who is able to do exceeding abundantly <u>beyond</u> what we could ask or think, according to the power that works within us, to Him be the glory in the church and in Christ Jesus to all generations forever and ever." **Amen!**

EPHESIANS 3:20

Messy In the Middle

I don't know about you, but I knew nothing about parenting. I was practically an only child as my only sibling was nine years older than myself, I never baby sat, and I was raised to be quite spoiled. A few years after Bill and I married, we found ourselves with a baby boy and as thrilled as we were at his birth, we were also overwhelmed with a responsibility for which neither of us felt prepared. When I say we knew nothing, I mean NOTHING!! It's surprising Kelly survived. He was our guinea pig for the other two children.

At the time he was born there was no such thing as disposable diapers and bottles. I was such a fiend for cleanliness. After all, didn't the Bible say, "Cleanliness was next to godliness?" Believe me, I searched the Scriptures for that particular "scripture" once I gave my heart to the Lord. I wanted to prove to others why it was so important to have everything spotless! In case you don't know . . . there is no such scripture. What a disappointment that was to me. Now how could I defend my compulsive behavior over everything being spotless?!?

Kelly sucked a pacifier. We couldn't get along without them. If one dropped on the floor I would never put that nasty thing back in the mouth of my precious son, so I had a sterilized jar full of sterilized pacifiers and they went in his sterilized mouth. Well, that part might be an exaggeration! Then we had Kayla and again, the sterilized pacifiers kept in the sterilized container until I noticed that Kelly who no longer sucked his pacifier would suddenly be sucking on his little sisters' pacifier or she would take her pacifier out of her mouth and stick it in his mouth. Now, I could not control this situation because they would do this and I would only discover it later. But I did notice neither of them died or got a disease.

Then along came Kyle, our third and last child. By now I was tired. I didn't have the energy or the time to do all that sterilizing of everything and I began to notice these kids were all healthy in spite of my "neglect." In fact, at that time we had a little dog and occasionally I would find the dog sucking on the pacifier! What was a mother to do?

RELAX!!! This was a word foreign to me at the time.

I read somewhere that the trouble with being a parent is that by the time you're experienced you're unemployed. In a sense that is true, but now with grown kids, grand children, and even great-grandchildren, I see that we're always parenting, but not the same way. Looking back on those years when our children were still under our wing, we made a lot of mistakes. I have dealt with a lot of regrets, a lot of "if only's." How about you? Are you living in the past of "if only I had done this, if only I had said this, if only I hadn't done this or that?"

"If only" takes so much energy. We are focusing on those things that we have no power to change. There is nothing we can do about the days that are already behind us. When we are living in the "if only's" it robs us of today. It makes us a prisoner of our past. Life has no rewind!

After we surrendered to Jesus, we realized we could not live back there with our regrets. Yes, we had failed royally in so many ways and now the only thing we could do was to humble ourselves and ask our children to forgive us in those areas where we failed as a parent. From time to time I would remind them this was our first time to be parents. Thankfully, they have been more than willing to forgive us.

As I mentioned earlier, Kelly was the last one to surrender to God's wooing. I think because the other two were younger, their hearts were more pliable and open, but unfortunately there was that season when they chose to explore the things of the world. Had Bill and I been wiser and more healed, perhaps our children would not have strayed from the Lord. We were both so immature in so many ways and we parented out of much fear, rather than trusting in the Lord. Because we had both been rebellious and headstrong, we parented our children as if they too would do things they shouldn't do. Also, at that time Bill and I both needed to know more about the loving nature of God. You see, we see God as we are, not as He is. We saw Him as the hard taskmaster, not the loving Father that He is, and as a result we raised our children in that type of environment. We were living under the Law, not under the grace Christ provided.

I'm only reflecting on these things in the hope that you might be spared some of the heartache we experienced, but we held the reins of our children much too tight and for much longer than we should. As parents we have a season where we need to give our children direction and then there comes a time where we need to allow them to make decisions based on the things we have taught them. In the Jewish home when a boy turns thirteen they have their bar mitzvah, or bat mitzvah for a girl. This is a religious ceremony celebrating their coming into the age of responsibility. No longer are they

Children need positive role models rather than critics.

---

considered children, but are now recognized as young adults. Since they are still in the home, they have the protection of their family to help them if/when they fail in decision making. Many Christians now have similar celebrations for their children to acknowledge their coming of age. It can be a very beautiful time and help the young person transition from one stage to another.

Another way we failed is that we were much too critical of our children. Children need positive role models rather than critics. Without sounding as if I'm making excuses, that was more or less the norm for parents when our children were still at home. We seemed to think too much praise would puff them up. We were much too critical of them. As I said earlier, look for the gold, not the dirt. Encourage them, as we all need encouragement.

In today's society we have another extreme in which parents rarely say anything negative to their child, It's like the pendulum has swung in the extreme opposite direction and there needs to be a balance. And as you probably know, it's not necessarily the things that are said, but also the way in which they are said!

I was a perfectionist at the time I was raising my children. After all, they were a reflection of me, right?!? So I had to make sure that they looked perfect and acted perfectly. Now, you might pride yourself on being a perfectionist but I have learned that it was out of my own insecurities that I tried to control everything and everyone. Once again, there is a balance. As God has brought healing into my life, I am not so hard on myself or others. Believe me, it is a much easier and relaxing way to live.

When Kelly went to college, he chose a school in another state. I have to admit I was happy to have him out of the house. I found I could be a much better Christian when he was not around. He seemed to bring out the worst in me. Know what I mean? However, I think of the Scripture in Matthew 15:18 that says, *"the things proceed out of the mouth come from the heart."* If that is true and we know it is then I can't blame Kelly for my actions, can I? I have to take full responsibility for the way I react. But, at this time I was not owning up to my own feelings and reactions.

Kelly had been away at school for several months and came home one weekend. We had a rule in our home, if you were there you went to church with us on Sunday. This was a strict rule. I have to admit, at that time in our life we were probably more religious than in relationship with Jesus. Today I hate being religious! Some of you may have gasp when you read that so allow me to explain what I mean. Being religious is what man can do and it's mainly based in works. It is man reaching up to God! It all depends on what I can do to gain His favor; praying a certain amount of time, more Bible reading, going to church every time the doors open, giving because we have to, and so on. There is nothing wrong with any of this, but it becomes legalism when we feel we have to do this in order to be a good Christian. We don't want to live under the Law. Jesus came to fulfill the Law and now it's not what we do, but why we do what we do. It's the attitude of the heart.

In relationship it is what Christ has done for us, His reaching down to us—all about grace, not works—*"not as a result of works, so that no one may boast."* (EPHESIANS 2:9) In relationship we do these things because of our love for the other. What a difference there is between being religious and being in relationship. When we do things because we have to, resentment can begin to build up. But when we do things from a heart of love, we grow and the other person can also grow.

Okay, back to Kelly coming home. When he got out of the car rather than hug him and tell him how glad I was to see him, I immediately started being critical of him. At that time Kelly had very curly hair, tight curls, and the afro style was "the thing." Kelly had grown out his hair and it was in an afro. I was livid! While he was at home he wore his hair the way we wanted him to! The first thing I thought of was, "oh no, he will be going to church with us. What can we do?" It was too late to take him to the barber.

Believe me, I was nervous. After all, Bill and I were now teaching classes called, "God's Ideal Family" and here was our son that looked anything but a part of the ideal family, or what I thought he should look like. Seriously, I was considering feigning illness Sunday morning. After all, I had my reputation to think of! Well, I was not sick and I had to go to church. I must also tell you what Kelly wore to church that morning. He had trousers that were a light shade of peach, or a very faint shade of pink and his shirt was black, sort of a shiny fabric and the shirt had a print of flowers or something small in the same color as the trousers. At that time men always wore socks, but Kelly had wedge shoes and wore them without socks. His hair was at an all time high that day. He had one of those combs that he used to lift the hair up and believe me it was high and lifted up! And if that wasn't enough, while at school he had acquired an Indian bead necklace with feathers between each bead—a feather, a bead, a feather, a bead, and so forth. So, God's Ideal Family piled in the car and headed for church!

We had not been attending that church too long so many of the people did not know our oldest son. Bill and I deliberately headed for the front pew as we knew Kelly would want to sit in the back of the church so he could exit quickly. With that we sighed a big sigh of relief. After church we took our time talking to everyone, allowing Kelly time to get out the doors. A friend that I did not know well at the time came up and said, "Oh, I saw your son this morning." I said, "Oh, our youngest son?" "No," she said. "I saw your oldest son!" I said, "How did you know he was our son?" And this was the shocker!! "Oh, Elaine, he looks exactly like you!" Have you ever been nailed so quickly?!? I could just see God up in the heavenlies pointing down *and she thought she would get out of there without anyone knowing!* Yes, He was having the last word.

I have told that same story for many years and in many places and always people roar when they hear this story. I agree, it is quite funny, but here is what happened soon after that morning. I began to feel terribly convicted for my attitude. Holy Spirit was showing me my heart. I realized I was full of pride. I also knew my son probably sensed the way I was feeling, my embarrassment, etc. Then I felt Father God begin to speak to my heart.

"Elaine, I loved you long before you looked right, or before you dressed right. I loved you when you did not act the way you should. I loved you when you were so rebellious. I loved you when you ran with the wrong crowd. I've always loved you. Nothing you did or would do kept My love from you. And Elaine, it was this same love that drew you to Me. Elaine, love covers a multitude of sin."

You see, God was after my heart. All this time I thought it was Kelly that needed to change, and he did, but bottom line, God wanted his mother to change and once my heart got right then I would begin to see my son the way God saw him. A very hurting, wounded young man. Even now as I'm writing this I am overwhelmed with how horrible my attitude was at that time. I was so filled with pride and didn't even know it. I've heard it said, "pride is like bad breath, everyone knows it but you." I love the scripture that says, *"It's the kindness of the Lord that leads you to repentance."* (ROMANS 2:4) Yes, it hurts, but it is so freeing when we agree with Father God!

Kelly went back to school and then decided he did

not want to return for a second year. I prayed and prayed about this, but you see, God had another plan. Kelly came home for the summer and I was really being tested. I was trying so hard in my own strength to be good. One evening Kelly, Bill, and I were sitting at the table just having a little discussion. I have no idea what it was about, but my button got pushed and the old Elaine came forth in all her anger and I screamed out at Kelly. Immediately I knew I had blown it and, as I said, I was trying so hard, but you see, my heart needed changing and only Jesus could do that.

I was embarrassed, scared, and ran upstairs and crawled in my closet. I didn't want to see anyone. I fell on my face and started begging for mercy. Up to that time it seemed we were making some steps forward in our relationship and in one moment my tongue had wiped out all the good that had taken place, or so I thought.

I cried out, "God, what can I do? How can I remedy this? With my mouth I have blown it! Help me!" And I thought I heard the Lord say, *"Go to your son and ask his forgiveness."* I got very quiet and said, "God, that's plan A. What is plan B?" And He said, *"There is no plan B!"* Now, I have to tell you this was almost like asking me to walk on water or cross the Grand Canyon without a safety net. This was so beyond anything I had done. It was not my nature and that is the thing; it's His nature and He is changing us from the inside out. I can't tell you how difficult that seemed in my understanding. As I've already mentioned, in my family where I grew up, we prided ourselves on never having to ask for forgiveness.

We just tossed everything under the carpet, acted like nothing happened, walked on lumpy carpet, and went about our business. In time we would forget it, but ask for forgiveness? Unheard of! In every argument Bill and I had he was always first to apologize. But you see, God was teaching me His way, not the way I did things.

I knew what I had to do and I was scared beyond scared. Courage? No, I was a wimp, a wet noodle, but I also knew that I would have no peace until I obeyed what God was telling me I must do. In a few minutes I heard Kelly make his way up the stairs. My heart was beating so fast I was sure I might have a heart attack. I jumped up, ran out to him before I could back out, threw my arms around this young man and began to weep uncontrollably and said, "Kelly, would you forgive me?" And then he said, "Mom, I was wrong, would you forgive me?" This was the beginning of healing in our relationship. Was it easy,? No! Was it right? Yes!!! Kingdom living for the most part is the direct opposite of what the world teaches.

The world says, take and God says, give. The world says, do it to others before they have a chance to do it to you. God's word says, "Do unto others as you would have them do unto you." The world says, hold on. God says, let go. God's word says, if someone has anything against you, go to them. The world says, they can come to me. God says, if they want your shirt, give them your coat too. God says, bless those that persecute you. Bless your enemy. All this is Kingdom living!

Kayla began to move away from God while in high school. She was working and becoming more independent

Living Expectantly

and began running with the wrong crowd. Looking back I can see where we held the reins much too tight. She was mature for her age and was capable of making good decisions, but out of fear we tried to control her every move. Eventually she rebelled against that. One day in prayer I felt the Lord lead me to a scripture that brought me much solace. It's found in Jeremiah 31:16–17. It's definitely the prayer to pray for those that have backslidden. *"Refrain your voice from weeping and your eyes from tears; for your work shall be rewarded, says the Lord, and they shall return from the land of the enemy, And there is hope for your future," declares the Lord, and your children <u>shall return</u> to their own territory."*

I have to tell you, when I discovered that scripture I let out a Hallelujah Howl! As believers, we are in covenant with Almighty God and His promises are for us. When He speaks a Word to you and you know that you know it's from Him, that is a rhema word. Hold onto that word until it comes to pass. At that time she had been away from the Lord for almost five years. Those were five long, long years, but we kept praying and be-

The world says, hold on. God says, let go.

---

lieving. I knew that I knew she would return and sure enough, it wasn't too long after getting that word that our daughter returned to her own territory. Like the prodigal in Luke 15 her heart was turned back to her Father!

And then there was Kyle. He was our baby and we all babied this fellow. Again, we were too strict and every thing was a no! Kyle was a thinker, and he wanted us to explain things to him, not just say, "because we're the parent and we said so." I'm not sure exactly when he began to wander from the fold. Sometimes it can be so subtle. Once he was in high school we saw a big change in him and out of desperation enrolled him in a Christian school thinking this would change him. It didn't. In fact it seemed he was drawn to kids like himself and they were there too as their parents were hoping the Christian school would change them. But God was faithful and eventually Kyle returned.

I had stood on Scriptures for both Kelly and Kayla and I wanted a fresh promise from God. I wanted to know beyond a shadow of doubt that God was speaking to me. During the years that I had prayed for our children I had discovered many different scriptures for the family and the children but now I felt I needed a fresh word. At this time Bill and I were living in Seattle. Kelly and Kayla were married and Kyle was living on his own. I had come back to Columbus for a business trip and got to spend some time with Kyle. Seeing him made me realize how far his heart had strayed. His countenance looked dark. I was concerned.

I kept asking God for a fresh word. One day I bragged and said, "God, I know all the scriptures to stand on for the children. I need a fresh word." I left Columbus with a heavy heart. I wanted my son to return to his own territory. As I got seated on the plane headed back to the west coast, I opened a little book that I often traveled with. It was small and I could easily toss it in my purse. It was only the New Testament. As I settled back in my

Living Expectantly

seat I opened the book at random, not looking in any particular place but wanting something to soothe my pain and give me hope.

Isn't it funny how we can read things in the Bible over and over and then suddenly see something and think, "I don't ever remember reading that." That's because it is the living word. It is alive and God knows exactly what and when we need to read something. For whatever reason I turned to the second book of Timothy and started reading the second chapter. Let me share this with you.

> *"Be humble when you are trying to teach those who are mixed up concerning the truth. For if you talk meekly and courteously to them they are more likely, with God's help, to turn away from their wrong ideas and believe what is true. Then they will come to their senses and escape from Satan's trap of slavery to sin which he uses to catch them whenever he likes, and then they can begin doing the will of God.*
> II TIMOTHY 2: 25–26 (LIVING BIBLE)

I sat there and was excited because now I knew how to pray for Kyle; that he would come to his senses and escape from the snare of the devil. But I also saw where I needed to change the way I approached Kyle: be humble, gentle, courteous. I don't know if you are aware of this, but God has such a wonderful sense of humor. As I was thinking on that scripture I felt He said, "You may know all the Scriptures, but you don't know all the versions." He was right. Reading from the Living Bible spoke so clearly to my heart.

At some point, Kyle called and told us he had been attending a church in New York where he was now living. A friend had invited him. I tried to not allow my heart to get too excited lest it would not last and then I would have to deal with disappointment. We were in the throes of moving back to Columbus. Shortly after we moved back, Kyle flew down to see us. I opened the door and immediately my heart began to leap with joy. Kyle's face was so changed. His countenance was alight with the presence of God. And I knew before he spoke a word, our prodigal had returned to his own territory! Are you where I was at one time, is it your heart that also needs to change? If so, give God permission to change your heart and watch what He does.

I have to brag on my children. They are wonderful! God has blessed us in so many ways. They are people of integrity and sound character and they, along with their wonderful spouses are all serving the Lord. It could have been so different considering our past. I can't tell you how grateful I am. God truly outdid Himself when He began the work in our home! I give Him all the praise and glory! Everyone had given up on us, but God. He didn't do all these things because we are so special. He did all these things because He is so special and He wants the same for your family.

After Kelly finally surrendered to the Lord he eventually became a pastor. After 12 years he stepped down. He is an excellent Bible teacher! I'm amazed at the nuggets he gleans from the word. He and Kimberly are building a website in hopes of ministering to couples as they have learned so much through their own experiences. They have four grown children and four grandchildren. Kayla is the mother of five children, (two are twins) and she and Mark have one daughter that is already in heaven. They have two grandsons. Kayla is very gifted and creative, and thanks to her computer knowledge she has helped her illiterate mother get this book written. Kyle married later and now he teaches art at a university in Florida and is making a name for himself as a portrait artist. He and Sara have five children and Sara home schools these children. It's amazing! Their children are the same ages of our six great grandchildren. We are now a family of four generations. A family renews itself with each new generation.

For those of you that are reading this book and you have loved ones for whom you are praying, be encouraged! God loves them more than we are capable of loving and yet He is waiting patiently for them to bend their knee. Ask Him for promises you can stand on, make them personal, put the person's name in the Scripture, and declare them over the person and the situation. (Job 22:28) says, *"You will also decree a thing and it will be established for you."* (NKJV)

Looking back on what I have just shared with you, it looked pretty messy in the middle. That's the way things are sometimes, but it doesn't mean that God is not working on your behalf. Sometimes it takes time to untangle a mess, but God is so good at that and it is exactly what He has done with our family. Several of our grandchildren are serving the Lord and for those that are not at this time, we are declaring the promises of God, *"You and your household shall be saved!"* (ACTS 16:31)

LIVE EXPECTANTLY!!! Look beyond what you see in the natural, arm yourself with His promises and watch Him reset the start button to *"Old things passing away and all things becoming new."* (ISAIAH 42:9)

Learning to Lean On Him

Not only were we learning to pray for our children and our families, but we were also learning that God was concerned with the smallest detail of our lives. I love the scripture in I Peter 5:7 in the Amplified. "Casting the whole of your care—all your anxieties, all your concerns, once and for all—on Him; for He cares for you affectionately, and cares about you watchfully."

Stop and think about that for a minute. That speaks volumes to us. He, Almighty God, cares for you (put your own name here, make it personal) watchfully and affectionately. Father God is not an absentee father as you may have grown up with. He is alert to your needs. He is vigilant, He never slumbers or sleeps. He is aware of EVERYTHING that concerns you and He does this lovingly, tenderly, and with great affection.

I love the ways of God. He begins to show us in small ways how we can trust Him and then as we learn to trust His nature and his character, our faith level increases and we are able to trust Him in other ways and in bigger things.

Think of Abraham, our Father in Faith. All through the scriptures when we first begin to learn of Abram

Learning to Lean On Him

(starting in Genesis 11) he was learning to trust a God he knew nothing about, a God he could not see. He was not brought up in a Christian home, his father Terah served other gods and worshipped the sun. And yet Abram left the home and land he was familiar with to follow an unknown God. Eventually his name was changed from Abram to Abraham.

During these years of Abraham coming to know God, he was also learning to trust God. Frankly, reading of his life it seems he was being tested throughout the Scriptures and now in Chapter 22:1 it says, *"after these things, that God tested Abraham."* What were all the other things that were going on in his life? Trial runs? Whatever they were, Abraham was learning that God was trustworthy and in his most severe testing or trial, Abraham was willing to lay his only son, the promised one, on the altar and sacrifice him, if necessary because He had come into a place of trusting and knowing that God was faithful.

You see, God takes us from small steps to giant steps in our faith. I believe He has great things in mind for each of His children, but He is looking for faith! And what is faith? Simply believing what God has said; taking Him at His word. He is not a respecter of persons. He is wanting to do great and mighty things in each of our lives. We should learn to live a life of expectancy, asking God to show Himself strong on our behalf.

I'm sure we have all said at one time, "It was a miracle!" when something took place that we thought could not or would not happen. To whom do you give credit at times like that? Do you think it was luck, chance, fate, karma—or was it God?

As a Christian, I choose to believe these miraculous things are from the hand of God. And I choose to believe in an expectancy of miracles! With God, all things are possible. I want to share some things with you that I believe only God could have done.

Probably the first miracle that I personally experienced was shortly after I gave my heart to Jesus. I've already mentioned how my husband and I were headed for divorce court. Let me share a few things leading up to that point. I was a very mixed up young woman. I saw no meaning to life, no purpose to live except to raise my children. I was just trying to survive in a frantic situation. I lived on tranquilizers and cigarettes. I smoked three packs of cigarettes a day. My children became so concerned about hearing the ads on TV that smoking could endanger your life, that they would hide my cigarettes from me. I was a total wreck, my home was falling apart. I had continual thoughts of suicide. Life, as I knew it and had experienced, was too hard!

I sought counseling before we finally saw a Christian counselor. Being a very proud individual I had tried unsuccessfully to change myself and my marriage, but things were too far gone. I needed help. That was when I turned to counselors and from some of the advice they gave me I'm certain they did not know the Lord. Their advice was: First, I never should have married in the first place, I was too emotionally immature as was my husband. As the counselor informed me, two emotionally immature people seldom are able to have a successful marriage.

The second piece of advice I got was just as depressing.

With my personality at that time being so terribly high strung and quite a perfectionist, they said I never should have had more than one child. Well, that information came a little late. I had three children. Which two do I get rid of? Obviously, he was unable to help me. This case was too far down the road to turn around, or so he thought.

The third piece of advice I got was to learn how to hypnotize myself so I could become more calm and patient. At that time I didn't have the money to purchase a very large and expensive book. He wanted me to read this book and start practicing the techniques. To tell you the truth, I was afraid of that type thing and looking back, I see the hand of Holy Spirit keeping me from getting the book. Hypnosis is not of God. If you have delved into something like that, simply ask God to forgive you.

Another piece of advice suggested I have an affair. This counselor thought it might build up my shattered ego. HELP! My nerves were ragged, I was a wreck. What was I to do? I needed a miracle and I needed a wise counselor.

After all these unsuccessful attempts of seeking counseling, I did what I should have done all along. I cried out to God and He heard and He answered me. Am I saying counseling is wrong? No, not at all. We finally found a good counselor, and we believe this man was sent to us by God. He was an answer to the prayer I had prayed.

As I have already mentioned, we had a miracle! I had a divine intervention in my human affairs. God came on the scene and that was the beginning of getting us on the right track to life. You see, life without God has no purpose or meaning. Oh, you might think it does and it might for a season, but eventually no matter how much success you have, no matter what accomplishments you have had, at some point you will realize there is still a void and believe me, nothing can fill that void except Jesus. I know, I have been there.

The God that I had been running from and avoiding has made such a difference in my life and the life of my family. I began to understand that this was a God that wants to be involved in my life. He loves me and cares about the smallest, most minute detail of my life. Early on I learned to pray simple, childlike prayers, just trusting that my heavenly Father cared and wanted to help me.

I recall the time my mother and her best friend, Dorothy, had come from Texas to spend some time with us. They were both very creative women and could sew

> **My prayers were simple, not eloquently spoke, but they were from a very sincere heart and I believed God cared.**

and design almost anything. I don't remember what they were making, but the sewing machine broke down right in the middle of the project. As I have already stated, my prayers were simple, not eloquently spoke, but they were from a very sincere heart and I believed God cared. My pastor often will say, "If you don't know who is doing what, just remember that God is good and the devil is bad!" Well, to me, having that sewing machine break down right in the middle of the project was not a good thing, so it could not have come from God. So, with my simple, childlike faith I laid my hands on that sewing machine, said to the enemy, "Take your hands off this machine in the name of Jesus," and immediately the sewing machine began to whir.

Later, Dorothy's daughter told me when Dorothy came back home she was trying to explain to Barbara what had happened and she said, "Barbara, she even prayed over that sewing machine and it started working!" By now family and friends were beginning to think I had become somewhat fanatical and I had. I was marked by excessive enthusiasm!" That is Webster's definition for a fanatic. I had become crazy about my God and believed what He said.

Kyle, our youngest son was mowing the lawn one day when the lawnmower suddenly stopped working. Well, he did what he had seen us do. He laid his little hand on that lawn mower, prayed over it, and told ole' slew foot (the enemy) to get lost and that lawn mower began to purr like a kitten. More than likely you are beginning to think this old gal is crazy, loony, or whatever. Actually I am more sane than I have ever been at any time in my life.

I love to decorate and sometimes I bite off more than I can chew as they say in Texas. Another one of my Texas vernacularisms, but I would imagine you aptly understand what I mean, right?!?

At this time, back in the 70's—people were using a brick-like material to apply on walls. Actually, though it was an imitation it looked very much like the real thing. I decided I wanted to brick a wall in our kitchen to give it a new look. Bill and I went to a lumber yard and found just what we were looking for. I can't tell you how excited I was! I have to say, Bill never seemed to get as excited about these projects as I did because he knew who would be doing the grunt work. I got the vision and he was to carry it out. And he did . . . reluctantly!

In order to apply this brick, you used a mortar type substance that you mixed with water. Simple enough, right? So, here we are in our kitchen and I could already picture the end result in my mind. I knew I was going to make our kitchen so warm and cozy and would totally change the present appearance. After all, I was the visionary in this project.

Bill had applied about half the portion of brick when he said, "We don't have enough mortar." Thinking he was only being negative because I had him doing something he really was not enthused about, I didn't pay too much attention to his complaining. But, it wasn't long until I realized he was right.

Ever the optimist, I reminded him that we could always go and buy more mortar. We jumped in the car, rushed back to the lumber yard, told the salesman what we were doing, and what we needed. Immediately he said, "Oh, I'm sorry but that was a discontinued product and I don't think we have any more supply in the back."

Whoops! Didn't figure on that. Bill immediately reminded me that we never should have started this crazy project to begin with and for a moment, a silent moment, I agreed with him. The salesman came back carrying one lone package of mortar in his hand. I was elated! Need I tell you, Bill was not. After all, he was the one doing the dirty work and he had already used several bags so he knew one bag would not be enough.

I am not one easily deterred when there's something I want to do. I am like that bull dog digging for the bone he knows is buried somewhere in the ground. He will dig and dig until he finds it. That is me! That morning I had just read the account of Jesus feeding the multitude with only five loaves of bread and two fish. Not only did He feed over 5000 hungry men, women, and children, but the Scripture tells us they had many baskets left over. (MATT. 14:17) My faith was high and now it was time to put that faith into action. *"Faith without works is dead."* JAMES 2:17 Okay, let's get to work!

I began sharing that scripture with Bill. He certainly believed what the Word said, but was not convinced that God would do the multiplication miracle for us. It's one thing to be hungry and need food, but it's another to want to change the appearance of a room. Because Bill is a good sport and wanted to make his wife happy, he went along with me. While he stirred the mortar I prayed and prayed some more. I'm sure you've already guessed the end of this story. Yes, not only did we have enough mortar, but like the Scripture we had some left over. You see, I was learning from these little lessons that God is the God of much more.

A friend of Kayla's had a dog that the entire family loved. One day we "happened" to be at Kathy's house when this dog came running up the porch and was bleeding like a "stuck hog" (another one of those Texas slang sayings.) For those of you who don't understand, that means a whole lot of blood was coming out of this dog. Kathy, being a young mother with several small children and a husband that worked long hours in order to put food on the table and provide the necessities said, "We can't afford to take this dog to the vet. What am I to do?" We asked if she would mind if we prayed for their pet.

By now we had gained the reputation of being a "little different." Not only did we pray about broken-down appliances, things we needed, now we're going to pray for a pet. I heard someone say one time, "How can you take up God's time by praying for such foolish and insignificant things?" As I have already stated, we were learning that if it concerns us, then it concerns Father God.

Bill and I quickly laid our hands on that little dog that by now was bleeding profusely. I wasn't sure that he might not bleed to death. Bill immediately thought of a scripture from Ezekiel 16:6, *"I saw you squirming in your blood and I said to you, Live!"* Now, he kept saying this over and over to the little dog. "Live! Live!" And wouldn't you know, he did. The blood immediately stopped and that dog took off running as if nothing had happened to him.

These are all simple things that I have shared, certainly nothing that would be earth shattering, but God was using these things to show us His nature and how much He does care about the smallest things in our life.

The Storm

We had left Texas because the company Bill was associated with had transferred him to Ohio. We knew one day this would happen, but we had hoped it would not be this particular state. We had nothing against Ohio, but we desired to be closer to our families. Unfortunately once a territory opened up, if you refused to transfer your chances of advancing in the company were slim and then it could take years to get another territory.

Bill is a born salesman. He loves people and they love him and trust his honest face and his slow, easy mannerisms. He is never one to push his ideas on another, but at the same time he has a way of convincing them they need this product. His territory consisted of two states, Michigan and Ohio. His product was not the most popular or desired thing in these states at the time, but gradually doors opened and people were buying these western boots and leather goods. But, on the negative side he had to travel five days a week in order to service such a broad area. He stayed with the company for almost eleven years and became one of the top five salesmen in the United States.

During these early years of being in Ohio and Bill traveling so much, neither of us minded as we really did not get along well enough to be together so in a way his

The Storm

time on the road was a respite for both of us. After the Lord got hold of our lives, our relationship was beginning to change and we actually were desiring to be together more and we were seeing how Bill's absence was affecting our children and it was not good. They needed their dad and I needed my husband. We began praying that a door of opportunity would open for Bill and he could switch companies.

Prior to this we had purchased a larger home as we were outgrowing our present house. Our mortgage was higher, but still affordable. At the time we were shopping for a house the economy shifted and loans were becoming harder to obtain. We ended up having to put more money down than we had intended, but having already sold our house we could not back out and did not want to. Kelly was in his first year of college so we had that expense, but we were not worried. Things were good and Bill was making good money, all commissions, but he was doing well. Eventually, people in this area were catching on to the western attire, sales had increased, and more doors were opening.

We were still fairly young in the Lord, but Bill was asked to teach a Sunday School class at our church. I was still teaching my classes to women and more doors were opening for me to speak in churches, at retreats, and some conferences. Although Kelly had not made a commitment to serve the Lord, we were confident that this, too, was coming soon. Another door finally opened for Bill to leave the company he had been with and we felt this job an was answer to our prayers. It looked like a very promising future for us and again, it was in sales with commissions and bonuses. This was Bill's niche! Men tend to be more adventuresome and he was excited about this change, this challenge. Women tend to be nesters, we want and need that security of a home, but I was going right along with him believing that this was a God thing. Could life have been any better?

Bill had not been with the company very long until he began acting quite strange and much different than his normal self. He seemed to be very distant and withdrawn, even depressed. As long as I had known Bill I never knew him to be depressed. This was very unlike him. Each day he seemed to withdraw more and more into himself. Was he worried about his job? He wouldn't talk about anything. He would come home, sit in a chair, and stare out the window. This unusual behavior went on for a number of days and I would tell myself he was probably worried about his job as we had talked about his sales not coming forth the way we had expected. But, I was also confident in God that this would soon come to an end as we had been praying so much.

During this time I received a call from his boss and he asked me if everything was alright with Bill. Not wanting to expose or uncover Bill's strange behavior I said everything was going well. He then proceeded to tell me that some of the people in the office had found Bill asleep in the car several mornings when they would pull into the private parking area. And then he told me that only that morning he had gone into Bill's office and found him with his head on the desk and Bill was sound asleep.

I was becoming very alarmed. I couldn't imagine

anything being physically wrong. Bill was young, seemingly in good health, strong and kept active by often playing golf, his favorite recreation. Days dragged on and now Bill was no longer even attempting to go in to the office. How much longer could I keep covering for my husband? What if he lost his job? What about our house? I was afraid. Where was God?

A good friend and neighbor suggested he call a doctor friend and see if this doctor would make a house call. He wanted to do this in a non-threatening way so as not to frighten Bill. I agreed and he called the doctor and he said he would drop by after a football game where he was the doctor on call. Dr. V. came over, checked Bill's vital signs, asked him some questions and had a little conversation and felt everything was okay, but he did tell me privately if I was still concerned about Bill the next day he would admit Bill to the hospital to observe him and possibly run some tests.

That same evening Bill was restless, nervous, and seemed to pace back and forth, back and forth. He would get up and then get back in bed, get up and then get back in bed. I finally moved to another room so I could get some rest. Sometime in the night, Bill burst into the room, demanded to know where I had been, and who I had been with. He was furious and I saw a side of Bill I had never seen. Suddenly, I was afraid for my safety and also the safety of our children.

The next morning I knew I needed to get Bill into a hospital and have him checked out. Our friend came back to the house to check on Bill and seeing how nervous Bill was he agreed we needed to get help right away.

I knew Bill would never agree to go to a hospital, so we pretended that the four of us would go and get a pizza. By now Bill's behavior seemed totally erratic! We pulled into the emergency entrance of the hospital and immediately Bill knew we had tricked him. The look on his face was so puzzling and I knew he didn't understand why we were there and why I had taken him to this place. He was angry at all of us and making threats that he would not stay in this place. It was one of the hardest things I have ever had to do, but I also knew he was ill and needed help. I had to entrust him to God and trust God in all of this.

This was in the 70's and not all hospitals were equipped with some of the advanced technology that is available today. Only one hospital in our area had a CT Scan machine used to diagnose disorders of the soft tissues of the body and the brain. The hospital where the doctor had sent Bill was not equipped with this scanner so he had to be taken to another hospital by ambulance in order to have this test. At first they thought he might have encephalitis, an inflammation of the brain. He was placed in isolation while they checked him out. Numerous tests were run and still they had no idea what they were dealing with. The unknown can be so foreboding. Knowing what you're dealing with, though it may be hard, at least you know what it is and can get the help that is needed, but the unknown can be such a mystery and your mind can begin to race with all kinds of thoughts of what might be.

Being so young in the Lord this was quite a difficult thing to walk through, but by now we had so many that were standing with us in prayer that we never felt alone. From the beginning of my salvation experience I had learned to turn to the Scriptures to find solace. I knew these were not just words on a page, but they were living words, it was God speaking to me. I was discovering so many promises that were available to me as a believer. I like to think of it as an insurance policy and I read it to find out my "coverage."

I happened upon Psalm 103. The second verse really stood out to me that day. *"Bless the Lord, O my soul, and forget none of His benefits; Who pardons all your iniquities; Who heals all your diseases."*

Sometimes we are not even aware of our benefits. I would think when starting a new job the first thing you would want to know is, what are the benefits? And yet, as Christians often we are totally unaware of the benefits God has promised us as His children. We knew He pardoned our iniquities, but now we were learning He also promised to heal all our diseases. Not some, but All!

Another Scripture that became a lifeline to me was is found in Psalm 27:13–14. I memorized this Psalm and kept quoting it to myself and over Bill. *"I would have despaired unless I had believed that I would see the goodness of the Lord in the land of the living. Wait for the Lord; Be strong, and let your heart take courage; Yes, wait for the Lord."* This is a promise that we will see the goodness of the Lord now, in this lifetime, not having to wait until we get to heaven. I looked up the Hebrew meaning of "wait" and it means to wait expectantly, eagerly look for it. In other words, wait, believing that something good is going to happen. ***LIVE EXPECTANTLY!***

We have learned that many times God will put us in a waiting season. It's not always comfortable, but God knows what is necessary. When you lift weights you build body muscles, but in God's "wait" training we should be building spiritual muscles. Because we live in such an instant society, we want everything to happen immediately. We don't have to wait for the oven to heat or for a meal to cook, we can just pop it in the microwave and it comes out instantly. We can send an email anyplace in the world in a matter of seconds. We don't have to get out of the car to open the garage, we don't have to get out of our chair to change the TV—just push a button and immediately our need is met. Who wants to wait? Give it to me, not later but now!

Several years ago when one of my granddaughters spent the night with us, I told her I was going to go downstairs into our basement as I needed to exercise on the treadmill. Of course she wanted to know why I was going to exercise and I said, "Because I need to lose some weight." She followed me to the basement, got in her little chair, and began to follow me with those brown eyes. I'm going as fast as I can on the treadmill and her eyes would move back and forth, back and forth. Finally growing very impatient as she had sat there all of five to ten minutes, she said, "You might as well quit. You haven't lost any weight!" And isn't that like most of us? We want results and we want them NOW!

As difficult as it was, we knew God was with us but we couldn't help but question why this was happening to us. Had we done something to lose God's favor? It was hard. Bill seemed to be losing touch with reality. He was now sleeping constantly. He woke for meals and then would go right back into a deep sleep. He was talking out of his head much of the time. Days had turned into weeks and still the doctors were puzzled by his condition.

The very day Bill was admitted to the hospital our income ended. Having only worked a short time and being paid by commission, we now had nothing. Keep in mind we were in this new home, our mortgage was more, our son was in college, and we still had two children at home. How were we going to manage? Looking at this in the natural it did not look good. In fact, it looked like a nightmare. However, faith does not see

> **Faith does not see things as they are, but how God declares they will be. This is kingdom living.**

things as they are, but how God declares they will be. This is kingdom living. If I told you I never doubted I would be lying. Every time I got my eyes off Jesus and on the problem I would become totally overwhelmed with the impossibility of our situation. I would wallow in unbelief one minute and self pity the next, but eventually would come back and get my eyes on Him.

One thing really helped me during this time, and as you know we really didn't know too much about the things of God. But God had been training us and we were learning that God was trustworthy, that He cared about the smallest detail of our lives, and He had already proven He was faithful. I didn't know too much about the character of God, but one thing I did know and I knew this in the very depth of my being. He loved me. He loved my husband and no matter what was happening He was not going to hurt or harm us. That seems simple I know, but it was one of the most helpful things that I did for myself during this time. I kept reminding myself that God loved me, Bill, and our children, and He was going to help us during this time. He had good plans for our life.

'For I know the plans that I have for you,' declares the Lord, 'plans for welfare and not for calamity to give you a future and a hope.' JEREMIAH 29:11

The Storm Continues

The pressure was building and the winds and waves of this situation seemed overwhelming. At times I felt we were sinking, but as always, God led me to a wonderful Scripture. I wrote it down and kept reading it over and over. I was able to memorize it and continued to quote it to myself continuously.

"Do not fear, for I have redeemed you; I have called you by name; you are Mine! When you pass through the waters, I will be with you; And through the rivers, they will not overflow you. When you walk through the fire, you will not be scorched. Nor will the flame burn you. For I am the Lord your God, The Holy One of Israel, your Savior." ISAIAH 43:1–3

I knew God would do something to encourage me, these things kept me going. Little by little I felt my faith was growing because I was seeing the hand of God in so many ways and His love was continually enveloping me. I continued to read the promises of God over Bill daily. He never gave any indication that he even heard them, but I knew his spirit man was hearing so I did not give up. I have found that in learning to trust God, it is never learned in comfort, ease, or without difficulty.

The Storm Continues

By now the doctors had determined Bill had a brain tumor. Those were the words we dreaded hearing. The doctor showed me an x-ray and his words to me were, "This is insidious and we must do everything we can to remove this or he will die!" Of course he was suggesting surgery and I did not want my husband to go through this. I was still trusting that God would just heal him. As we all know, any type of surgery can be risky, but especially the opening of the brain. The decision to do the surgery was up to me. I couldn't even consult with Bill about this as he was incoherent much of the time. I had so many people trying to give me advice. I knew for the most part they all meant well, but it was becoming confusing. One group would say, "Don't put him through surgery. I knew someone that died!" Another would say, "Just keep trusting God to heal him without surgery." I finally opted to give the doctors the go-ahead. According to the doctors, time was running out and Bill was not getting any better. I have since learned we cannot box God in. He uses many different means to heal. It was in His hands. This was my husband, but he was God's son and He alone knew the plan He had for His son.

A few weeks before we actually found out Bill had a brain tumor I felt God dropped something in my heart—a question I was not expecting. "Elaine, even if I choose not to heal Bill will you still trust Me?" It was one of those times that I knew that I knew this was God and He was confronting me with this question. Would I still trust God? I knew it would do no good to blithely say, "Sure Lord, I will trust you no matter what!" It was one of those things that I needed to ponder in my heart.

I needed to weigh this mentally. Would I still trust Him, could I still trust Him?

I don't remember when I finally gave Him my answer, but I do recall it was not in a short time. I seriously thought about this and when I finally talked to Him about it I knew in my heart it was an honest answer and I said, "Lord, even if you choose not to heal Bill I will still trust You. It does not negate who You are. You are the healer." I believe in doing this it was a total relinquishment on my part, a letting go, totally surrendering to God, but trusting Him no matter what. God is always after our heart and sometimes our attitudes are not right and we come to God in a demanding posture of feeling it's our right and God has to do what we say. In letting go it has nothing to do with a lack of faith, but it is saying, "God, I trust You and the outcome is in Your hands."

The three young Hebrew boys mentioned in Daniel 3 were a perfect example of trusting God no matter what. You know the story, but in the event you have forgotten let's look at that Scripture. A decree had been established and every time the people heard the sound of certain instruments they were to fall down and worship the golden image that the king had set up. The young Hebrews would not bow or bend their knee to this image. They were God worshippers, not idol worshippers. Someone tattled on them and told the king they were disregarding this edict and not bowing as they were told to do. Nebuchadnezzar was raging when the boys were brought before him and told them if they did not bow down they would be cast in the midst of a furnace of blazing fire.

The Storm Continues

The young men answered him and said, *"If it be so, our God whom we serve is able to deliver us from the furnace of the blazing fire; and He will deliver us. But even if He does not, let it be known to you, O king, that we are not going to serve your gods or worship the golden image you have set up."*

Now the king was filled with wrath. Even his facial expression had changed and he gave the order to heat the furnace seven times hotter than they normally heated it. And now for the rest of the story. The young men were cast into this blazing hot furnace and were tied up with their own clothing. The king was astounded when he looked in the furnace and saw four men, not three. He knew that their God was there with them and protecting them. Whatever happened, the young men knew their God would be faithful. He would either deliver them in the fire—through the fire or from the fire—and into God's arms. Whatever God decided they knew they were not alone or forsaken.

I will not go over the entire rest of the story, but I love this part and I must share it with you in the event you have not noticed this. Nebuchadnezzar was so proud and boastful. In verse 15 he said, *"What god is there who can deliver you out of my hands?"* But now we see that something has happened in the heart of the king. In verse 28 he is blessing the God of Shadrach, Meshach, and Abednego. He has visibly seen the young men walking around in the fire, they have not been harmed, the fire has had no effect on their bodies, their hair was not singed, their clothes were not damaged, and even the smell of the fire was not on them.

The king knew that fourth person in the furnace with them was no ordinary person, this was a divine being and this being was mightier than any gods Nebuchadnezzar knew about. At the end of the chapter the king is aware that these young men were supernaturally delivered because they had put their trust in their God. And now the king made another decree: if anyone says anything offensive against the God of these three men they would be torn limb from limb and their houses reduced to a rubbish heap! Why? Because the king realized *"THERE IS NO OTHER GOD WHO IS ABLE TO DELIVER THIS WAY."* What way? **He allows us to go through these horrendous trials and still causes them to turn out for our good and His glory.** That's the God that I serve. Not only were they delivered from the things binding them, but they also received a promotion! Keep in mind, anytime we go through a difficult time and pass the test, keep our attitude right and etc. We are promoted! We will come into another level of faith!

Bill and I were fairly young Christians at this time but reading about the Hebrew young men, I decided that I wanted that kind of faith. I wanted to trust God no matter what. If He delivered the Hebrew boys, could I trust Him to deliver us? The promises are there for us, can we believe that He will do what He says?

I have learned through the years that faith in God lies in tension. Standing in faith, believing that God will do what He says requires a person to live confidently between the problem and the promise. First we have the promise (the Word) next we have the problem (the trial) and then we have the provision (that which was promised).

The Storm Continues

Think of Abraham and Joseph. They each had promises that God had spoken. Abraham was promised a son from his own body and yet many years passed before this was fulfilled. In the natural it looked impossible. Joseph had a dream where his family would bow before him. The brothers hated him, his father questioned him about this (GENESIS 27) and then years passed. His brothers wanted to kill him, they sold him into slavery, he was in prison. All of these things that were happening seemed to contradict everything that both men thought would happen.

In Psalm 105:19 we read about Joseph, *"Until the time that his word came to pass, the word of the Lord tested him."* You see, Joseph's greatest trial was the word he had received, the dream, the promise. Sometimes the word that we believe God has spoken to us can be quite confusing as it doesn't seem to turn out like we thought and this is where the tension is. Faith is always believing without evidence. And our expectation of God is what determines our level of faith. Can we trust Him, will we believe what He has told us? Can we wait patiently for the promise to be fulfilled, or will we be like Abraham and do our own thing to make it happen? Abraham leaned on his own understanding and because of his age and the age of Sarah he felt he had to do something to help God out. (GENESIS 16)

Isaiah 50: 10–11 warns us of the danger of making our own light when we are walking in darkness. There are times when it seems God has not heard us, is not answering our prayers and we do something to try and make it happen. That was exactly what Abraham did. Today we are still reaping the results of Abraham's decision. Man-made light can be deceptive. I understand how difficult it can be having to wait on God. And that is why there is tension between the promise and the provision. But there is a reward in waiting on God's perfect timing.

Bills' mother and stepfather had come up from Texas. At one time his stepfather was president of an insurance company and the first thing he wanted to do was examine Bill's life insurance policies and make sure everything was in order. His mother had even purchased a dress for the funeral in the event Bill did not make it through surgery. There was such a battle going on. I was doing everything to keep believing God, to hold on to His promises. But with all these other things that were so contrary to what I felt God was wanting to do there was a battle. Who was I going to believe?

By now Bill was seldom coherent. If he did speak it never made much sense. One morning, a few days before the scheduled surgery, I walked into his hospital room and he seemed very alert. He told me that in the night he sensed an angel of death in his room. He said, "Honey, I could smell death all around me!" Then he said, "But God spoke a scripture to me in the night." And Bill quoted this scripture to me verbatim. Now, this was very unusual as Bill had never been one to memorize scripture. Remember when Jesus spoke to Simon Peter and told him the devil had demanded permission to sift Peter like wheat? Then Jesus told Peter that He had prayed for him that his faith would not fail. That part was familiar to both of us, but here was the part that neither of us remembered when we would hear people

The Storm Continues

quote that scripture . . . *"But when you return, go and strengthen your brothers."* Oh my! That was a rhema word from the throne room of God. Number one, it was such a miracle that Bill remembered it and could quote it and then the second part—the really good part—*"go and strengthen your brothers."* Bill shouted, "I am not going to die. I have a job to do. I must strengthen my brothers." And another thing, Jesus was saying to Bill, *"Bill, Bill, I have prayed for you,"* not Simon, Simon. Jesus was making this scripture very personal to Bill.

On the morning of surgery, Bill's mom and I drove to the hospital together. Several of our friends had gathered to stand with us and pray during the surgery. Several of them also felt led to fast. Believe me, they were holding up our hands like Aaron and Hur held up the hands of Moses. (EXODUS 17:12) The doctor told us surgery would take several hours and as soon as they were finished he would come out and talk with the family. Shortly after that, before the surgery, the doctor called and asked us to come up to the surgery area. My faith was at an all time high. God had spoken that scripture to Bill and now the doctor wanted to see us. In my mind I was cer-

I took one look at his face and I knew something had happened. I knew whatever news he had to tell us was not good.

tain they had done another x-ray and the doctor was going to tell us the tumor had disappeared. When we arrived in the area where the doctor was waiting for us I took one look at his face and I knew something had happened. I knew whatever news he had to tell us was not good. His countenance was downcast. The doctor proceeded to tell us he had taken another x-ray and said, "this does not look good at all. We are not even sure we can get in there and do anything." This was not the report I was expecting. I looked at him and said, "Then what are you doing to do?" The doctor answered, "We have no choice but to open him up and see if we can do anything."

This was a huge blow. I was not expecting this at all. Without thinking I grabbed the hands of the surgeon, lifted them up to the Lord, and I began to pray a prayer of sheer desperation. I asked the Lord to give this doctor wisdom from on high, knowledge to know what to do, and to guide and direct his hands throughout the surgery. Had you known Doctor L. you would have known this was totally inappropriate. When Bill went in to the hospital we had no idea who to get as his doctor. But the staff highly recommended this particular neurosurgeon. We later learned this guy was the BEST! But he was very impersonal. It was difficult for him to speak the layman's language. In no way was he warm and friendly. He appeared cold and aloof, but again, he was considered the best! I was totally intimidated by this man, but when one is desperate, one will do desperate things. That was why I never gave it a second thought to reach out and pray for this man. He needed help and though we knew God was in charge, He was using this doctor to accomplish His purposes for His son.

Bill's mom and I returned to the waiting room. My heart went out to his mother. I knew she was afraid for

The Storm Continues

her son. After all, this was her only child. I tried, as did others to console her and offer her comforting words, but what is there to say at a time like this? The time seemed to pass so slowly. The unknown was like a dark veil wrapped around us cutting off our breath. We all continued to beseech heaven on behalf of our loved one and after what seemed like unending hours we were notified the doctor would be down shortly to talk with the family.

When the doctor finally arrived, I could tell by his face he was not bearing good news. He said, "We were unable to remove the tumor it was so deeply imbedded in his brain. Had we tried to remove it he could have been blind and paralyzed, and it was malignant." My mind was saying, "No, this can't be. He can't die. God, You told him he had to strengthen his brothers." The battleground was my mind at this time. What will I believe, who will I believe? I gained a semblance of composure and asked the doctor how long he thought Bill had? He answered, "Right now he is fighting like a tiger and only time will tell."

We went back to where our friends were waiting. They were all such wonderful and close friends, they loved Bill like a brother and it was very difficult to tell them what we had just heard. After I shared the report from the doctor I could see the hurt and pain in their faces and I can't explain this, but something rose up in me and I determined at that moment I was not going to give up, no matter what the doctor said. My God would have the final word!

The doctor friend who admitted Bill to the hospital

was becoming such a source of encouragement to us. He would come into Bill's room from time to time and always had an uplifting word. We knew they were continuing to run tests on the biopsy. One day Dr, V. ran into the room and seemed so excited. He said, "They are downstairs wrangling (the word he used) over the biopsy." They had run several tests, had even sent the biopsy out of state to be tested, and now they were arguing and disputing over the report. Later that same day Dr. V. rushed into the room totally out of breath and said, "You have had your miracle. It is not malignant!"

Perhaps at this point you might be saying, "Well, it probably wasn't malignant in the first place or the doctor made a mistake when he said that to begin with." Maybe so, but frankly I don't think so. I believe somehow, at some point, God changed the biopsy in order to confound the doctors. Dr. V. was on the scene from the beginning and his report was, "You have had your miracle."

Years later I happened to receive an email from a nurse that had been on duty at the time Bill was hospitalized. She was a Christian and we had briefly talked during this time. Unbeknownst to me, she knew someone that I knew and years later we corresponded by email for a short time. I was very excited to hear from her as I had questions that I wish I had asked at that time, but had not. I started asking her a lot of questions and though it had been a number of years since the incident she did remember a few things. I asked her about the biopsy report. Fortunately she vividly remembered that time. She said there were other professionals around the nurses' station who stared in disbelief at the report. No one knew what to think and yet, the report read, "benign." That was wonderful news!

But as wonderful as that was, according to doctor the tumor was still there. Remember, it was too deeply embedded in the brain to try and remove it, and if you recall, the doctor had told us in the beginning without surgery he would die. So, he was alive but it was still a very serious situation. However, we had that rhema word that Bill would return to go and strengthen his brothers. Knowing this, we were assured the tumor was no big deal for our God who had parted the Red Sea, caused bitter waters to be made sweet, raised the dead, caused the lame to walk and the blind to see. To God that tumor was like a period on a page . . . the end! We were getting a close up view of this God that we had only read about in the Bible. He was revealing Himself to us in a very personal way.

After forty-two days of being confined in the hospital, Bill was finally released to go home. I can't explain it, but I knew Bill would not die prematurely. I knew God had something more for him to do and the word Bill received confirmed this. But what we didn't know was the battle

> **You need to know, once you decide to trust God and declare His word, the thief will come and try to rob from you.**

ahead. We were about to enter into something neither of us knew anything about. We were about to get "on job" training. You need to know, once you decide to trust God and declare His word, the thief will come and try to rob from you. He does not want us to come into that place of victory that Christ provided. He will oppose you on every corner. But God had purpose in this. We were about to learn something about warfare.

The Wilderness

We were celebrating now that Bill was back home. It seemed like an eternity since he had been with us in our home and he was equally happy that he was finally released from the hospital. God had been so good to us, but we were drained from all the pressure. We were anxious to get back to a normal life, but we weren't sure what normal would be considering the tumor was still there and Bill no longer had a job.

Shortly before Bill had become ill, I had come upon a Scripture that I continued to read over and over again. Little did I realize at the time how that particular Scripture would become a "lifeline" for me in the days ahead. This was the book of Deuteronomy, in chapter 8. God was preparing the Israelites to enter into the Promised Land. They spent forty years on a journey that really should not have taken more than eleven days.

I kept reading this chapter for some reason and one thing that caught my attention was in verse 2 where God talked about this wilderness. Up until this time I had heard nothing about a wilderness. Now that Bill was ill, I felt God was speaking to me through this book in the Old Testament. wilderness is defined as; *A bewildering situation.* I would attest to that. We were in a very bewildering situation. Why was this happening to

The Wilderness

us? We loved God. We were telling everyone that came across our paths all that God had done, how wonderful and faithful He had been to us. We began to question ourselves. Had we offended God in some way? And it is never wrong to check our heart but we also need to remember that the devil is the accuser of the brethren and we soon realized that he was accusing us and wanting to make us doubt God and ourselves.

I soon learned that the wilderness can be our "school." The wilderness can be a training ground for us. In the wilderness we can learn things about ourselves and also about God. The first lesson God wanted the Israelites to learn was found in verse 3. *"Man does not live by bread alone, but by every word that proceeds out of the mouth of God."* In that same verse it says, *"He humbled them. He let them be hungry. He fed them manna which they did not know."* We needed to learn that **God is our source!**. He gives us resources in order to meet our needs, but bottom line, God is our source!

When I read *"He humbled them, tested them to see what was in their heart,"* that puzzled me because I kept thinking, "God, You know we love you. Why are You checking to see what is in our hearts?" But, it wasn't for Him to know. He already knew our heart. He wanted to show us our own heart. And trust me, He never allows us to see the ugliness of our own heart to shame us or put us down. He only wants us to agree with Him and say, "Yes, Lord, I see that and unless You change my heart in this area I am stuck here. "Change my heart, oh Lord." And He will and He does! Never will He shame us.

In a wilderness period He is checking our commitment.

Living Expectantly

Are we only serving God because of what He can do for us, or are we serving Him because we really love Him? Our relationship with God must move from a "contract faith" (I'll follow God if He treats me well) to a relationship that transcends any hardship we might encounter. Each of us must learn to develop a relationship with God apart from the circumstances of life.

We didn't know at the time, but God was about to thrust us into a place of total dependence on Him. But, haven't we all been taught that God helps those who help themselves? Listen to me; if you were taught that and you believe that, renounce it. That is a lie! We did not realize how prideful we were until we were in this place of having to totally depend on God for everything. As I had already mentioned our income had been totally cut off, but in this school of the wilderness we were about to learn how God was able to meet our needs. He was going to reveal Himself to us as **Yahweh yireh . . . the Lord will provide!** This was the "manna" we knew nothing about that would come down from heaven to meet our needs. God began to stir the hearts of His people. Some people we knew, some, we had never met, nor heard of, but these people heard our story and started sending us money. It was incredible! We had never seen such generosity, and especially from people we did not know and some did not know us, but were aware of our need.

It was winter and each of our three children needed winter coats. Need I tell you there was nothing in the budget to cover this need? Why? There was no budget! We had depleted every visible means we knew of to find money. So, as I had already been learning, I had to turn to prayer and I asked God if He would supply our children with these much needed winter coats. I was learning through all this, God has His own "ways and means committee." I thought some generous Christian would hear from Holy Spirit that our children needed coats and would send the money, maybe anonymously—that would be less humbling. Know what I mean? I would soon find out that was not God's plan.

The house we had purchased earlier was in a very nice neighborhood. In fact, at that time it was one of the nicer areas in our community. We lived on a cul-de-sac and there were still several homes to be built. To our knowledge there were only a few Christians living in this neighborhood. One evening someone rang our doorbell and it was a couple of our neighbors whom we knew were not Christians. They were so excited to share why they had come over. They had brought an expensive ham and we could also see an envelope that seemed to be bulging with cash. They were eager to tell us they had taken an offering from the neighbors and here was the money and ham they had collected. I was totally embarrassed. To think they knew we had a need was terribly humiliating to me at that time. And if that wasn't enough, Bill was so excited that he lifted the envelope up to the Lord and said a prayer of thanksgiving for their generosity. Oh My! Now I was really embarrassed. Now they had evidence we were crazy fanatics!

It was all I could do to keep that phony smile on my face until they left. As soon as they went out the door I rushed upstairs and cried my heart out to the Lord. Why, I asked Him, did You allow them to do this? And I felt

He said to me, "Excuse Me, didn't you recently pray about coats for your children?" Well, yes, but I certainly did not expect it to come this way and especially from non-Christians." And then I felt He said to me, "I will use anyone and any means to meet your need. That is not for you to decide." Now, I was beginning to see my own heart. I, who thought I had no pride, was filled with pride and He was allowing it to be exposed. And I must tell you this; there was enough money given to us from this group that enabled me to purchase lovely coats for each of our children. We were learning who God is and how He was able to take care of His own.

Things were beginning to feel more normal each day. During Bill's hospital stay we had received so much attention. People were visiting us, calling us, cards were daily being delivered to our home or hospital room. Even our mailman questioned why we were getting so much personal mail. Trying to explain to him all that had happened and how God was blessing us opened a door of opportunity for Bill to talk to this man about a personal relationship with Jesus. On our front porch, this man bowed his head and invited Jesus into his heart. God had blessed us in numerous ways, but now the activity seemed to be dying down and though we needed to get back to a more normal lifestyle and routine, we were beginning to feel a little neglected. One morning I said to the Lord, "God, do You see where we are?"

Later that morning Bill said to me, "Honey, I am so hungry for something." Thinking he was probably craving one of my homemade lemon pies, I asked him what it was he wanted to eat? After all he had been having a diet of hospital food for months. He said, "Honey, I can just taste pickled cauliflower and canned peaches. I would love some Del Monte canned peaches!" My first thought was, did they get something twisted in his brain during surgery? And why would anyone crave such a strange mixture of food?

Little did we know that God was about to use this for us to learn how involved God is in the smallest detail of our life and we would also be learning another lesson in humility. Often at Christmas time schools will choose a needy family in their school district and gather groceries for them; a beautiful gift for the needy family until

> **Little did we know that God was about to use this for us to learn how involved God is in the smallest detail of our life and we would also be learning another lesson in humility.**

you happen to be that needy family (especially if you're filled with pride). I'm sure you are one step ahead of me and know we were selected as the family in need. When word got to the school that someone in our neighborhood needed help they questioned if that was true. It was true and we were being targeted by everyone. Lessons in humility can be hard to learn sometimes especially when you are full of pride.

That same morning when Bill expressed the crazy things he was craving, we left to run some errands. When we returned we found several boxes and bags of groceries sitting on our porch. We could see they were filled to overflowing. We later found out the school had dropped these things off. We never found out who had turned in our name as the recipient of this good will. Probably just as well, right?!? I have to say, even though we were proud, we were not too proud to keep the groceries. We needed them!

As we dug through the bags we were overwhelmed with all the wonderful things that had been given to us. You would have thought someone had read our grocery list. As we got toward the bottom of one bag we lifted out a jar of pickled cauliflower, a can of Del Monte peaches, and even a jar of home canned peaches! With that discovery I burst out crying! I was so aware that God saw and was concerned about the smallest detail of our life. He had heard Bill express his desire for those particular things and He had miraculously sent each of them. When I said to Him earlier, "Do you see where we are," He was showing me that He did not miss one detail of our life. It was an incredible, life changing moment for both of us. We were learning that He was not just a historical Jesus, but He was a living, loving God that was our friend and wanted to be involved with our daily life.

I started imagining a scenario in my mind; a little boy suddenly remembers that he is to bring a canned good or something for a needy family to school that day. He is hesitant to tell his mother as they are about to depart for school and this is the last day to bring in something. "Mom," he says, "I forgot to tell you that I'm to bring something to put in the box for a needy family." The mother panics! Her pantry is bare. She has nothing to send. In fact, she was planning to drop her son off at school and then go to the grocery store. But suddenly

The Wilderness

it was as if a light bulb had gone off in her mind. "Oh, where did I put that jar of pickled cauliflower?" the mother asks herself. 'I know I still have it, but haven't figured out why our friend brought such an unusual thing to our pot luck. Good thing I didn't try to serve it. Where did I put it?" She anxiously dug around under the counter and there it was, that lone jar of pickled cauliflower. She felt it was okay to send that with her son. After all, no one would know where it came from and at least her child was able to donate something. Little did this mother know how God was going to use her unusual contribution.

This reminds me of the story of the mother that packed a lunch for her son: five barley loaves and two fish (JOHN 6:9). The young boy was going to the mountain where he heard Jesus might be. She was only doing what any mother would do. Little did she know how Jesus would use that to feed a multitude and the story would be told over and over again of how God was able to supply!

All of this was almost more than my mind could comprehend. I thought of the Scripture that says, *"The earth is His footstool, heaven is His throne."* ISAIAH 66:1 But look how involved this BIG GOD wants to be with His children. He is not an absentee father. Down to the smallest of details and desires, He cares. I was reminded of another story in Scripture that carries out that truth even more. I ran to find my Bible and looked in the concordance to see where the story was about the two sparrows. I found it in Matthew 10. Jesus was speaking to His disciples and trying to prepare them for persecution now that they were followers of His. He wanted them to trust and not be afraid, but to know that God knew everything that happens, even down to simple little sparrows. And if He was concerned about a bird, how much more concerned He would be for them. In other words, no matter what might happen, God wanted them to be aware of how valuable they were in His sight and how He delighted being involved in their life.

He used the analogy of the simple sparrow, though a sparrow wasn't of much value and would bring very little money, yet not one of them would fall to the ground apart from the Father's participating presence. And then He told them how the very hairs on their heard were numbered. When my husband hears this he always says, "Yeah, well what about those hairs I'm losing?" Rest assured, He is even aware of every hair that is no longer on your head. In verse 3 Jesus said, *"Therefore, do not fear; for you are of more value than many sparrows."* I was certain there was more to this story about sparrows than what I was reading so I started doing some research on sparrows. At the time this took place we did not have the resources for research such as the internet, or Google. At that time I was unable to gain a lot of information, but here is what I discovered.

First of all, a sparrow is a small, plain looking, dull singing, very dirty bird and regarded as a pest. This was about all the information I could find on these birds. With this knowledge, small as it is, what do you think He is trying to communicate to us? I believe He is saying, "Look, so what if you do feel totally insignificant, unimportant, and you can't sing, you have no talents,

The Wilderness

you've got a dirty past, and most people think you are a nuisance, a pest and don't want you around. Never mind what others may think, I love you with an everlasting love and thought you were of such value that I sent My Son, My only begotten Son, to die for you. That is how valuable you are to Me and My kingdom!

As difficult as this time was in this wilderness period, we were learning so much about God. At times I could imagine myself sitting in God's lap, being spoon-fed by Him. That was how near I felt His presence. I continued reading Deuteronomy 8 and in verse 3 it said, *"He humbled you and let you be hungry, and fed you with manna which you did not know."* I can't say we ever went hungry,

> **He was wanting us to know everything we had was coming from His hand, our source. We were to keep our eyes on Him and not to focus on our circumstances.**

but there were several times when we weren't sure how we would pay our bills, but He was wanting us to know everything we had was coming from His hand, our source. We were to keep our eyes on Him and not to focus on our circumstances.

Many times during this training period time we would find ourselves at what seemed like the eleventh hour questioning how we were going to pay a bill. Occasionally we would get a colored reminder that if it wasn't paid by a certain date, the utility would be cut off. I believe He allowed this in order to see what we would do. Would we wait on Him or would we lean to our own understanding and move in the flesh? Having lived this way I understand how difficult it can be to wait, but I have also learned waiting on Him is much better than moving ahead. Keep in mind not everyone is called to live like this, but we knew we were being trained and prepared for something in our future and God was teaching us His ways.

One time we had a particular utility bill that was about $46.27. Because this was a number of years ago this was not the exact amount, but however much it was, the exact amount came to us in the form of a check, down to the very last penny. It was amazing what was happening and we never told anyone our needs.

I love the story in II Corinthians 1:8–11. Paul was in Asia and in a very precarious situation. It was so severe, so out of their control, there was nothing they could do to help themselves. If God did not come through on their behalf they would perish. He said, *"We were burdened excessively beyond our strength, so that we despaired even of life; indeed, we had the sentence of death within ourselves."* The only thing they could do was put their trust in God. Paul did just that and then wrote, *"He delivered us from so great a peril of death, and will deliver us, He on whom we have set our hope. And He will yet deliver us."* Past, present and future! This was not the first extreme situation Paul had found himself in, but he knew from these other trials that God would be faithful. Have you come to a place in your journey that you see your trials as an opportunity for an even greater victory than you have had in the past? I believe our trials don't just happen randomly, but are designed to bring us into a deeper relationship with God. Let me ask you this, on whom have you set your hope? Often we depend on our own abilities and resources and only look to God at the times when we can't do anything. Some people turn to Jesus like they would a credit card, just there in case of an emergency. Since He is our source of everything, why not keep plugged in to Him at all times, rather than just in times of crisis or when needing a miracle?

Looking again at Deuteronomy, Chapter 8, I love the promises in verse 7–8. God is telling the Israelites that He is bringing them into a land of promise. *"A good land, a land of brooks of water, of fountains and springs, flowing forth in valleys and hills. A land where you shall eat food without scarcity, in which you shall lack nothing."* In other words, we have the promise that no matter where we are, what valley we might be in, what mountain we are trying to climb, what trial we are enduring, the wilderness, that dry place, that impossible situation, He is reminding us that better days are ahead! This trial will not last forever. It has a shelf life. Be encouraged and ***Live Expectantly!***

Jamie Buckingham is one of my favorite authors. He passed into Glory in 1992, but he will always be remembered for his hilarious wit, his uncommon insight, and his expertise in storytelling. He once wrote, "Real faith is laughing at life because we believe God is in control." That should help to remind ourselves of this truth. God is not the author of every thing, but God is Master over everything. We know He did not put the brain tumor on Bill, but we also know in God's economy He will use everything for our good and His glory. Bad things happen to good people, but for the Believer, we can stand on Romans, the 8th chapter and 28th verse. *"For we know that God causes all things to work together for good to those who love God, to those who are called according to His purpose."* Many people read this scripture and think God makes all things good. But that is not what is being said. God is able to take the worst things, the hardest places, the injustices of life, and etc. and somehow cause them to work together for our good. This is a promise for those that love God, the called!

The place we were in was definitely hard. It was a bewildering situation, that's for sure, but we were continuing to declare and believe Bill was healed even though that tumor was still there (according to the doctor). I remember hearing someone say that before God does a new thing there is usually a wilderness period. We knew by the Spirit that God was moving us into something new and better, but sensing that did not make the place we were any less difficult. There can be treasures in our greatest trials if we can see them from God's perspective. I love this quote – *The burden of suffering seems a tombstone hung about our necks, while in reality it is only the weight which is necessary to keep down the diver while he is diving for pearls."* RICHTER

We're diving for pearls.

Move That Mountain of Fear

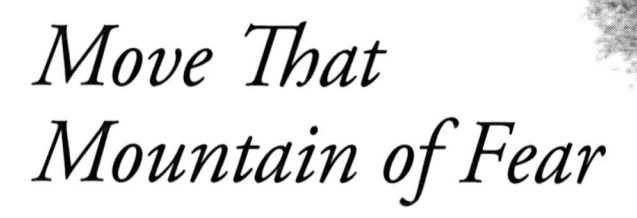

At the time this was happening, it was in the early 70's. We were in what came to be known as the Charismatic Movement. It was during this time that Bill and I had a personal encounter with Jesus Christ. People that never had read the Bible were beginning to read the Word. We started devouring the Scriptures. We took the things that Jesus said literally. According to the word, Jesus is the same yesterday, today, and forever. (HEBREWS 13:8). We had no reason to doubt that He would heal today just as He had healed when He walked the earth. He instructed His disciples to go and preach the gospel and certain signs would follow; they would lay hands on the sick and see them recover, cast out demons, speak in tongues, etc. (MARK 16: 15—18) We considered ourselves His disciples and we believed everything He taught in the word! I know

> **I have searched the Scriptures and found nothing to prove that the time of miracles ceased.**

Move That Mountain of Fear

many people today think that miracles were for then, but not now. I have searched the Scriptures and found nothing to prove that the time of miracles ceased. Just because we don't always see them doesn't mean they have ceased. Maybe the problem is within us. Perhaps we have quit believing. Could it be we are not living with the expectancy of what Jesus can do and wants to do? We took God at His word back then and we still continue to believe that what Jesus spoke while He was here on earth applies to us today. As for me and my household, we live expectantly!

People were following our story. People we didn't even know had heard about the word Bill felt Jesus had spoken to him that he was to go and strengthen his brethren, and they were watching and waiting for the outcome. Because of our testimony, we were being asked to speak at many places. Doors were opening for me to teach my classes for women and people wanted Bill to come and share his story. Much of the time when Bill would go out to speak, he would come under severe attack. Several times he would even be blind for a few minutes and sometimes unable to walk. This was new to us. We had no idea what was happening, but this we did know—it was not God. We realized this was an attack and the enemy was trying to discourage us and prevent us from sharing all God had done and was doing. And though we realized it was an attack, the symptoms were very real!

It came to me several times that Bill was walking in fear. I would question him and he would always deny that he had any fear. Quite often he would come back with the same answer, "Well, you're not walking in my shoes." And this was true. I could visibly see he was blinded at times and unable to walk, but in my heart I felt this was a spirit of fear that had attached itself to Bill. No matter how much I tried to convince him of this, the more he would deny he had any fear. The longer this continued the more convinced I became we were dealing with fear. I could sense such a heaviness in our house. At times I almost felt I was being suffocated. When I would leave the house, I always felt more free and lighter, but once I returned home it felt like something was trying to grab me.

One day we took our car to be serviced. At that time, the car dealership was located downtown. We dropped the car off and walked to a fast food place for breakfast. Bill was fine and we spent time in the place eating, drinking coffee, and enjoying a relaxed morning. About the time we got ready to leave, Bill said, "It is here!" By now we referred to this thing as an "it." I immediately knew what Bill meant and I could see his eyes begin to flutter and I knew he would either be blind or unable to walk, sometimes both things would happen. It was as if his legs turned to rubber with no strength in them at all, just loose and not connected. I helped him outdoors, leaned him against a building, and called a taxi to come pick us up even though we were within walking distance where we had left our car to be serviced. Bill could not walk!

When the taxi arrived I had to ask the driver to help me get Bill in the car. Seeing him, you would have thought he was drunk. He had no control whatsoever over his body. And whatever was happening was becoming more and more frequent. It was a nightmare and the symptoms were real, but I still kept thinking this was nothing more than fear. These things would come quickly and then they would leave just as fast and he would be normal again, as if nothing happened. It was all quite puzzling.

Then one night Bill had a very interesting dream. While dreaming, he actually raised up several inches from the bed and this woke him up. He later shared the dream with me. It was like God was speaking to him and said, "Bill, just as the enemy put boils on Job that were real, he has put symptoms upon you. Though they appear real, they are not. They are a lie!"

At this time, Bill had been appointed as president of one of the local chapters of the Full Gospel Businessmen. This group met monthly at a hotel and always had guest speakers that would come and share their testimony. For one of the meetings, Bill had invited a doctor who lived in our state, but another city, to be the guest speaker at one of the dinners. This doctor had a well-known reputation of moving in a keen sense of discernment and word of knowledge. That evening as the meeting was starting, Bill got up to make an announcement and "it" hit! Bill was blind. The other leaders and the doctor gathered around Bill and prayed for him and then "it" left. Later than night after we had gone home and were asleep, Bill awoke to go to the bathroom and could not walk without my help.

He shook me awake and I had to help get him into the bathroom. Bill said, "In the morning I am calling my doctor. I feel I am going to die." After I got him back to bed and settled down, I was unable to get back to sleep. Many thoughts were going through my head. Yes, I could see the symptoms, they were very real and it seemed as if life was being sucked out of him, but I still kept feeling this was nothing more than fear!

After a very sleepless and restless night, I finally got out of bed and felt I should try to talk to the doctor that had spoken the evening before and see if God had shown him anything. All this was new to us; I needed someone to help me walk through it all. I was able to call the doctor and apologized for calling so early, but told him of our sheer desperation over the situation. I said, "Did God show you anything when you prayed for my husband?" He said, "As a matter of fact, He did." He went onto say, "As I started to pray for his healing, the Lord stopped me and said, "He is healed, this is a spirit of fear!" At last someone was confirming what I had been sensing for months. I told him what I felt the Lord had been showing me for so long. He said, "Let's agree in prayer that Bill will know the truth and the truth will set him free." He prayed a brief prayer with me and I have to tell you, I felt a huge load had been lifted off of me. Bill called Dr. L, the neurosurgeon the next morning and they were able to get him in the same day. By now this doctor had a CT scan in his own office. They ran the test and then we had to wait several days for the results. I never mentioned to Bill, my conversation with the doctor that had been the guest speaker.

Several days later, I drove Bill back to the neurosurgeon's office for the results of the CT scan. By now I was having to do all the driving and had been for quite some

Move That Mountain of Fear

time. I waited in the car until Bill came out. As soon as he walked toward the car, I could see a drastic difference in his gait. He looked more determined, almost angry! He quickly opened the door and said, "I have been duped!" I asked him what he meant? He said, "I have been believing a lie! The tumor is no longer there!" All that the CT scan showed was scar tissue where the tumor had once been. It was no longer there! Those were the sweetest words I had heard in a long time! God had removed the tumor! Now, there was also another miracle . . . I never said, "I told you so."

Bill said, "We are going home and we are going to make war on the enemy. We are going to take back what the enemy has tried to steal from me." Need I tell you how excited I was? We got in the house and put a record on. (Now you know how long ago this must have been. We had records back then, not CD's) This particular recording was by a well-known artist. It was nothing but songs from the Scriptures. We turned the volume so high that I think every neighbor for miles around heard. But we didn't care. This was a war cry and we wanted to make sure ole' slew foot heard.

We both paced back and forth, back and forth, throughout the house screaming at the top of our voices and yelling out the promises of God. We have since learned we didn't need to yell. God has given us the authority and power over the enemy, but at that time it seemed the most effective way to get rid of him. We continued to scream out these promises over and over: *"No weapon formed against us can prosper." "He has not given us a spirit of fear, but one of power, love and a sound mind."* *"Jesus said, 'it is finished.'"* After several hours of doing this—and it was several hours as there was a huge stronghold in our house—we finally felt freedom and peace. Bill looked at me and said, "It is gone!" And I knew he was right. I, too, felt the peace and release at the same time. Bill opened the closet door, took out the broom, and swept the enemy out of our home. *"And whom the Son sets free, he is free indeed."* JOHN 8:36

We are not recommending this as a magic formula for ridding your home of any oppressive spirits, but this is our story and this was how God led us. As you know from reading this or hearing it, fear is real, but fear is not, and never will, be from God. Do not allow that spirit to gain a foothold in your life, but deal with it quickly. Find someone that you trust and be honest with them if you are battling fear and get them to pray for you. Agree that the enemy must leave.

I'm sure you have noticed many times in Scripture how God would send an angel to say to the people, *"Do not fear." "Fear not." "Be of good courage,"* and so on.

Fear is real, but fear is not, and never will, be from God. Do not allow that spirit to gain a foothold in your life, but deal with it quickly.

Many times He would preface this before sending them into a place, warning them beforehand not to fear. Fear can be a natural reaction to things we have not walked through and even to those things we have already experienced, but it is never good to allow fear an entrance into our heart. Proverbs 4:23 tells us, *"Watch over your heart with all diligence, For from it flow the springs of life."* In other words: protect your mind, and emotions, and don't allow the enemy to gain any ground. If/when fear knocks on your door, send Jesus to answer the door.

After acknowledging the fear, Bill began to walk like a new person, a person with a renewed mind. No longer was fear a problem. The enemy knew we both recognized him and he did not try to come back. He had such glorious freedom once again. Knowing what we have learned through the years, we now see that fear had gained ground at the time of Bill's birth as he had a difficult birth. We are learning that even when the child is still in the womb, they can be very affected by their environment, emotions and that type thing. Fear was something Bill had struggled with occasionally, now fear eventually gained a huge place in Bill's heart when he would think about the tumor still being there and the possibility that he would die. He believed a lie! Even though Holy Spirit had spoken to Bill in that dream, *"when you return, go and strengthen your brethren,"* the lie was more real to Bill than the truth of God at that time.

We know God does not waste anything—even the bad things—but He will use these things to bring glory to Himself. This has been a testimony that Bill has been able to share throughout the years and as a result he has seen others be set free. Yes, it was hard, but we gained the victory and God got all the glory. *"But thanks be to God, who always leads us in triumph in Christ."* II CORINTHIANS 2:14 Because of the Cross and what Jesus accomplished for us on the Cross, we fight from a place of victory, not for victory! Do you understand the difference? The last thing Jesus said as He hung on the Cross was, *"IT IS FINISHED!"* (JOHN 19:30) Jesus had defeated death! He became our Victor—one that defeats the enemy—and we no longer have to be a victim or have a victim mentality. The victory has been won, not will be won, but past tense!

When we walk through any trial, the enemy is always wanting to defeat us, but we have to train ourselves to be spiritually alert. We must we aware of his tactics. Resist him as we read in I Peter 5:8. How do we do that? The same way Jesus did. Remind yourself and the enemy what God's Word promises! Trials prepare us for the coming blessings. In any trial, we can either grow or groan, we can become bitter or better. The "I" makes the difference. Choose life!

The Honeymoon Is Over

There was a visible difference in our home once Bill recognized it was the enemy trying to rob from him. No wonder God had said, *"He has not given us a spirit of fear."* II TIMOTHY 1:7 (KJV) That "it" that we kept calling this thing, was fear and we discovered how real fear can be and how it can incapacitate a person.

So much had been happening since we had moved into our new home that I had not even thought about decorating. But now my thoughts were turning to wanting to do some things in our home. We had finally gotten a lovely, large master bedroom with its own bath, but unfortunately there was not much money to do any decorating. I have to admit I was becoming out of sorts about this seemingly impossible situation. All I did was complain about what we didn't have, what we couldn't do.

At some point I attended a Women's Aglow retreat. This was a first for me to go to something like this and Joy Dawson, a well-known speaker and author, was the featured speaker. She had recently moved to the United States from her homeland of New Zealand. She told how they disposed of everything in order to move here. It was like starting over for them when it came to furnishing

The Honeymoon Is Over

their home. She said she began to thank and praise God for each and every piece of furniture they would be needing. She would thank Him for their beautiful sofa and describe the color and the style. She told the audience that her entire house had been supernaturally furnished. She had also prayed about a piano, but shared that she did not pray exactly the way she should have and rather than it being given to her, it was loaned to her, but she was thankful for it!

I'm sure by now you realize how that caught my attention. So, instead of complaining, which had accomplished nothing thus far, I started thanking the Lord for each and every thing I felt I needed in order to furnish and decorate that bare room. I must admit this was not always easy. In fact, it seemed sort of foolish to thank the Lord for something I did not have at the time. But, I was learning about the nature of faith. *"Now faith is the assurance of things hoped for, the conviction of things not seen."* HEBREWS 11:1

Daily as I made our bed I would thank the Lord for that beautiful coverlet with the lovely bed skirt, the throw pillows, and even a cute little roll type pillow. I thanked Him for the matching draperies and the matching tablecloth for the small, round table. Ginger jar lamps were very popular at that time and I thanked Him for the ginger jar lamp! No longer was I complaining, but I was actually seeing these things in my mind and thanking Him in advance.

One day I was with a friend and she was shopping for linens. I noticed a set of these beautiful sheets that were the perfect colors for our bedroom. In my heart, I knew these were exactly what I wanted to have the coverlet and draperies made from. I don't recall the brand name any longer, but it was a well known designer and the sheets were not cheap. I told no one about this, but I continued to pray and thank God for those particular sheets, and then I knew I would have to find someone that could make all these things for me.

My mother was a gifted seamstress. She could make and design anything and did professional looking work even though she was self-taught. Around Thanksgiving of that year, Mother called and asked if we had been able to decorate our bedroom. Of course I told her "no." Then she said, "I feel I would like to make you a bedspread and drapes, would that be all right?" I'm sure you already know the answer. YES! YES! Mother had excellent taste and she knew the colors of our bedroom so I knew I could trust her to come up with something very pleasing to my taste. I never mentioned the sheets I had seen or how I had been praying. I was leaving all of that to Father God. He knew! In the meantime, Mother became ill and was unable to get her shopping done or sewing completed by Christmas and she let us know it would come sometime later.

Kayla was in a youth group at our church and they were planning a retreat for the young people. She came to me one day and said, "Mom, I have got to have a new robe and slippers." Money was tight and I suggested she start praying for God to supply her need. As parents we are so quick to always supply things for our children as the needs arise. There is nothing wrong with that, but it is also good for them to learn at an early age to depend

The Honeymoon Is Over

upon God for themselves. This was an opportunity for Kayla to learn that God cares for those things that concern her. I'm sure Kayla thought it was much easier to ask Mom and Dad than to wait on God for His provision, but at this time she knew if she was going to have that new robe and slippers she would have to turn to God herself and that was exactly what she did. If I remember correctly, I believe it was sometime in February before my mother was able to finish her sewing project and get the gifts shipped to us. Kayla was getting a little anxious as the retreat was just around the corner.

Finally the Christmas box arrived. I tore into it so fast, paper and tissue were flying everywhere. I removed the coverlet from the tissue paper that it was carefully packed in and my mouth flew open. Here was a manufactured coverlet in the exact fabric of those sheets that I had seen several months before! I was speechless. As I continued to unwrap each thing, I found a lovely bed skirt and drapes that Mother had made that were the same fabric as the coverlet. Then I discovered two throw pillows and the adorable roll pillow I had described to the Lord. Next was the matching tablecloth for the small round table. Later Mother told me she had some scraps left so she sewed them together and made the tablecloth.

I can't explain how touched I was by all this. He saw, He heard. And to think my mother had no idea that this was the fabric I had desired. It was amazing how she was led by the Holy Spirit. Everything was there but the ginger jar lamp. At that time I really did not care. I was so overwhelmed with everything God had done, who cared about a lamp? But, I will tell you about that later.

Yes, I was elated to see how God was in all this and to see how personally involved He wanted to be in my life. As a child, I knew about God, but I did not know Him. There is a difference. I was now in relationship with Him! In James 2:19 we read, "Even the demons believe." So you see, it is not enough just to believe, but do you <u>know</u> Him? Are you intimately acquainted with Him? Or do you see Him as a hard taskmaster? Are you afraid to move close to Him?

A.W. Tozer, a well-known Christian author, made a wonderful statement that I want to share with you. "God is waiting to be wanted." Almighty God, Creator of the Universe, waiting to be wanted?!? By whom, for what? He longs to have fellowship with you, with me.

At one time, I saw God as that hard taskmaster, unloving, uncaring. Always looking for something to "nail" me with. As a little girl in Sunday School I can remember the teacher saying, "Now you must be good, for God sees everything that you do." Believe me, that brought me no comfort. In fact, it put much fear in my young heart and maybe that was where I began to think that He was this mean ole' god that cared nothing about me.

But let's turn that statement around. What if you would say to your young child when they ask you, "Does God see everything that I do?" and you reply, "Oh, honey, God loves you so much He can't take His eyes off of you!" Look at the different connotation that statement makes. You see, we don't see God as He is, we see Him as we are. As we begin to get healing in those areas where we are wounded, where we have fear and unbelief, we begin to see this loving God as He is. Tuck this away

The Honeymoon Is Over

in your heart . . . ***God is not mad at you . . . He is mad about you!***

Somehow I got sidetracked; I want to get back to my story of the Christmas box. As I told you, I had suggested to Kayla that she begin praying about that robe and slippers . . . I bet you already guessed. Yes, Mother had made Kayla a beautiful red robe and matching slippers. Mother knew nothing about the prayers Kayla had been praying over the past few months and Mother had never tried to make slippers until this time, but you see, God was leading her.

Now, lest you think God is like Santa Claus, or a vending machine, right there at your beck and call—He is not! However, He is concerned about those things that concern His children. Perhaps you are thinking, "Well, we are all His children so why does He allow this and that to happen if He cares so much about us?" Good question. Here's the answer: we are not all His children, only those that have been born again does He call His children. Yes, we are all His creation, but each of us have to make a decision to make Him Lord of our life. We have to acknowledge that we are sinners by nature and need a Savior to deliver us and free us from that sin, and of course, that is Jesus Christ.

We are volitional human beings with the power to exercise our will and make choices. Do you want Him in your life? Then speak up and tell Him so! Say something like this . . .

"Jesus, I need you. I recognize I am a sinner. I ask You to forgive me for my sin. Cleanse my heart. Make

Living Expectantly

me the person You created me to be. Thank You for hearing my prayer and changing my heart. May I become more like You. Please remove any false ways from me and begin to teach me Your ways. Amen!"

As new Christians, God teaches us Who He is, we learn more and more about His ways, it seems everything is good, all our prayers are being answered. Life is good, and when life is good we naturally think God is good, right? Isn't that the way it is in the early season of a marriage? You're deeply in love, but you're still learning about this person you married and you think nothing could change the way you feel about them. Then there may be a period when you begin to question why you even married that person. Things take a turn and life is not as easy and smooth. It can be the same way in our walk with Jesus. When something happens, something we don't understand, often we begin to question God or accuse Him.

I love the story of the first couple in the Bible, our relatives, Adam and Eve. Remember them? Let's take a minute and look at their story. In Genesis 2 we see that God formed man from the dust of the ground and God Himself breathed into the nostrils of this man, so that he became a living being. Then God planted a garden in Eden. It must have been an amazing sight. Everything was lovely and lush. There were no weeds to pull, no insects to eat away at the foliage and harm the plants. Adam didn't have to worry about drought or watering as a mist went up from the earth and watered the entire surface of the ground. Wouldn't we all like that kind of garden today?

The Honeymoon Is Over

God made man caretaker of the garden but commanded him by saying, *"From any tree of the garden you may eat freely; but from the tree of the knowledge of good and evil you shall not eat."* And He went on to say, *"For in the day that you eat from it you shall surely die."* (VERSES 16—17)

God saw that it was not good for man to be alone and He said, *"I will make a helper suitable for him."* I believe most of us know the rest of the story. God put man into a deep sleep and while he slept God removed one of his ribs, closed up the flesh in that place, took the rib, and made this gorgeous creature called "woman." And please keep in mind, this wasn't just any rib. I'm certain it was a prime rib! Adam woke from the deep sleep and imagine what he must have thought when he saw this woman. He might have questioned if he was dreaming. I'm sure this woman was a beautiful sight to behold. Try to picture this: Adam gazing at this creature God had brought him. He had never seen anything quite like her. Keep in mind he had just named all the animals, but he knew in his heart this was not one of those kind, this creature was of a higher species and he said, *"She shall be called Woman!"* Now I have a feeling he put a little emphasis on that word "woman" and it was more like this: **"Whoa! Man!!"**

This turned out to be a wonderful day and they were in love. But as we move into Genesis 3, we see that the serpent has now come on the scene. If you have walked with the Lord any length of time, then you already know once you receive a blessing it doesn't take long for word to get around to the enemy's camp and someone arrives on your doorstep to try to rob you of this blessing. In

Living Expectantly

this case it was ole' slew foot himself, the serpent!

He went first to the woman and said, *"Indeed, has God said, 'you shall not eat from any tree of the garden'?"* Too bad she communicated with him, but she did and she said, *"From the fruit of the trees of the garden we may eat; but from the fruit of the tree which is in the middle of the garden, God has said, 'You shall not eat from it or touch it, or you will die.'"* And the serpent said to the woman, *"You surely shall not die! For God knows that in the day that you eat from it your eyes will be opened, and you will be like God, knowing good and evil."*

Please pay close attention to what I am about to share with you as this is the genesis, if you will, of sin. This is

Anytime the enemy can cause us to doubt the goodness of God, then our entire perception of who God is will be a false perception.

---

the enemy's first attempt to cause man to doubt and question the word and the goodness of God. He was saying to her in a very sly and subtle way that God was withholding good from them since He had instructed them to not eat from one particular tree. Can you see this? And now he is telling her the benefit of eating from this tree. *"For God knows that in the day you eat from it your eyes will be opened, and you will be like God, knowing good and evil."*

Anytime the enemy can cause us to doubt the goodness of God, then our entire perception of who God is will be a false perception. Is He really good? Does He really have my best welfare in mind? Can I trust Him?

The Honeymoon Is Over

These are the things the enemy will try to use to cause us to question God and accuse Him.

Continuing in Genesis 3, we see that the woman took the fruit from the forbidden tree, ate, and gave some to her husband and he ate, too. God Himself had spoken directly to the man and yet he was disobedient. Now their eyes are opened, they saw that they were naked, and in order to cover themselves they sewed fig leaves together to hide their nakedness.

As I mentioned earlier, when we are in that "honeymoon period," nothing can change the way we feel about that person. But when something changes, what is the first thing we do? We start the blame game and this was exactly what Adam did when God confronted him. Adam told God, *"the woman whom You gave to be with me, she gave me from the tree, and I ate."* In other words: "Look, I was asleep. I have never slept like that. I awoke and there she was. I didn't ask for her. You brought her to me. It was Your fault, her fault, but not mine" So typical of mankind. In Texas we call that "passing the buck." At least the woman was honest and admitted she had been deceived by the serpent.

I have heard it said that in our journey with the Lord we have two significant experiences. The first one is often tender, gentle, delightful, loving, exciting, and etc. In this experience we see the manifest presence of God, His blessings.

Then there is the second experience which can seem lonely, obscure, quiet, a time of dry periods, and even dark periods. I have read that some people would refer to this as "The dark night of my soul." We might be asking, "Where is God?" Those are the times where He seems hidden.

Both experiences are necessary. The first I would call, "The Honeymoon period." This period draws us to Him. The second one teaches us about Him, who He really is. And it is in this time where we learn to walk totally by faith. This is a time when we have to rely on the promises of God found in His Word. During this time we cannot rely on our feelings, as they can be deceptive. As Christians we don't remain on the mountaintop forever. It's in the valley where the growth comes. Graham Cooke spoke at our church several years ago and I love how he described this. He said, "Manifestation is a time of blessing and when God seems to be hidden from us, this is a time of building."

Yes, we had been in that honeymoon period. It had drawn us to this wonderful, forgiving God, but now He was calling us into a deeper walk with Him. He was going to do some building as well as rebuilding, tearing down some things that were not of Him. Before constructive restoration could continue, false foundations had to be exposed and torn down.

Years ago, a well-known hotel chain built a new hotel in Michigan. It was an impressive building. From any floor you could look down and see the main lobby. There were glass elevators that were situated on the outside walls of each floor. On the mezzanine floor they had a gorgeous ballroom with exquisite furnishings. At that time there was nothing else quite like this building. It was a state of the art conception.

As beautiful as all this was, there was something not

quite right in the initial structure, but was not visible to the naked eye. It was only when they had a dance and many people gathered on the ballroom floor, that they realized the building was not made to bear all the extra weight and pressure. The floor collapsed and hundreds fell to their death.

After David had sinned with Bathsheba he wrote in Psalm 51:6, *"Behold, You desire truth in the innermost being. And in the hidden part You will make me know wisdom."* If you would look up the word "innermost" in the Hebrew concordance, the word is "tuchah" and then leads you to another word "tauch" and the prime word here means to overspread, overlay, coat, plaster over. "Hidden" in the Hebrew means concealed, closed, stopped up.

Hopefully you are getting the picture of what David was expressing as He cried out to God. He knew he had sinned. He never denied it, but he also had become aware that there was something deep within him that needed healing. He needed changing from the inside out. We may look good on the outside, we may know how to talk the talk, but when the pressures come, when adversity hits, will we be able to stand? Will we fall into sin as David did? Will we begin to question God? Some have even turned away from God in those hard places. Psalms 103:14 says, *"He Himself knows our frame."* That word "frame" means form, purpose, intentions. He knows the plan He has for us. He has a blueprint for our life. He is the architect of us and He alone knows what needs to be done in order for us to fulfill the plan, the purpose, and to enter into the destiny for which He has designed us.

Because He knows our frame, He knows the weight that we can bear. If you recall, Moses was in the wilderness forty years before he became the mouthpiece for God. Only God knew the pressures that Moses would experience as he led the Israelites across the wilderness. Jesus did not come into His ministry until He was thirty years old. During both of their lives they were being prepared. In those dark times, those hidden places, God is taking away and adding to our frame in order that we can accomplish His purposes upon this earth. When pressure comes, He does not want us to fall, He wants us to succeed. During that time of building, or rebuilding, in our life, He might need to pull us away in order to prepare us for what is ahead.

During the forty-two days Bill was hospitalized, our not knowing in the beginning what was wrong with him, having no income, and on and on and on, it was hard. It was what I would call a dark period in our lives, although God was doing so many beautiful things in our life. Through that period we learned a side of God we

As Christians it's not so much what we get, but what we are becoming. Are we looking more like our Father each day? That is the goal.

---

might never have known otherwise. I have to say I would never want to go through something like that again, but I would never take for granted the things we learned during that season. The difficulties of our journey can be our greatest teachers, and through these hard places we can become much stronger in our spiritual walk.

The Honeymoon Is Over

The book of Job is a very controversial book. Many scholars argue over why Job was tested in such a harsh way. In my humble opinion, it seems to me that Job lived by the letter of the Law as most people did during that time, but until that time of severe testing he had never experienced the grace of God. I feel the last chapter of Job explains what the trials were all about. In chapter 42,verse 5. we read that Job said, *"I have heard of You by the hearing of the ear; But now my eye sees You."* Job had an encounter with God and now He was seeing everything with new lens. He was seeing things from God's perspective and not his own. All God was wanting from Job was an admission of trust. What does He want from us when we are walking in places of hardship? An admission of trust. He just wants us to say, "God, I trust You!"

As Christians it's not so much what we get, but what we are becoming. Are we looking more like our Father each day? That is the goal. It takes much preparation to run the race that is set before us. We are not running a sprint, but a marathon. First we must learn to run a mile and with each mile we get strengthened for the next mile.

Dr. Lloyd Jones said it well, "The worst thing that can happen to man is to have success before he is ready." God is preparing you, whether you are in that honeymoon period with all those wonderful blessings or whether you are in that building process, both are necessary for where we will be tomorrow.

The Miracle of the Green Dress

Things were definitely better since Bill had been set free from fear, but we were still living by faith; in other words, trusting God to take care of our needs. Bill had not returned to work, we were ministering quite a lot and receiving love offerings, but we never knew what we would get, if anything.

In many ways it was very hard, but in other ways it was quite exciting. Just seeing how God was able to meet our needs was an experience in itself. We were learning He is our provider. The only bad thing, the provision didn't always come on our timetable, another area in learning to trust. If we started depending on something coming through the mail, it would not come that way. If we were looking to the love offering when we would speak, it would not come that way. We were learning we had to keep our eye on Him and no one or nothing else.

A good friend of ours who had a healing ministry was going to be ministering in Indiana. He had become a mentor to Bill and had taken Bill under his wing to

The Miracle of the Green Dress

train him in ministry. He was a first cousin of Lester Sumrall who was a well-known evangelist in Indiana and had a television station. They wanted Bill to fly over and share on one of the shows. Of course we did not have the money, but after praying about it, Bill felt he was suppose to go, so trusting if this was God, then He would provide. Bill made arrangements to fly there.

The day came for Bill to fly out; it was a Sunday. We had gone to church as he was scheduled to leave later in the day. So far no money had come in to pay for the ticket. When that happens you begin to question. Have

> **Just seeing how God was able to meet our needs was an experience in itself. We were learning He is our provider.**

we missed God? As we were walking out of church, a fellow that we did not know very well came up to Bill and said, "God told me I'm to give you this money." He placed some money in Bill's hand and it was exactly the amount of the ticket. Again, one of those miraculous provisions of God, but it didn't come until the eleventh hour, or almost the twelfth hour?!? But come, it did.

The Christmas season was upon us. All our bills were paid, we had groceries on our shelves, but there was no extra money for Christmas. From the time I was a young girl, Christmas had always been a big thing for our family and we had carried that into our family after Bill and I married. But here we were with nothing extra. I was getting more and more depressed as the days wore on.

Kayla and I had gone to the mall to pick up a few

essentials. She and Kelly were old enough to have little jobs and they had been buying a few things to put under the tree. A friend had cut a live tree from her property and brought it in for us to decorate. The tree was cheerfully decorated, but I can't say I felt very cheerful myself.

While in the mall, we walked into one of my favorite stores. It had been a long time since I had shopped for anything for myself. Browsing through the store, I went into the area where I normally would have shopped. They had just gotten in some beautiful things that were in a line of clothing that I loved. Long skirts and jackets were in at this time. I had two suits from this particular clothing line, one that I had bought and, one that someone had given me. The new ones that I was admiring that particular day had a long skirt and jacket, they also came with a blouse, slacks and vest. Beautiful five piece ensembles!

There were several different styles and different colors. I happened to love forest green so I took a set off the rack, drooled over it and thought to myself, "Will I ever be able to buy these type of things again?"

I placed it back on the rack, glanced at the price tag, and saw it was $164! Now, keep in mind this was in the 70's. Today something like that would probably cost several hundreds of dollars, maybe even a thousand. It was so beautiful. Under my breath, not speaking it out for anyone to hear I said, "Oh, Lord, I would love to have that."

Several weeks had passed and it was only a few days before Christmas. Our tree was still fairly bare when it came to gifts. We had a few things for the children, but

The Miracle of the Green Dress

Bill and I had agreed we would not give each other a gift. We needed new tires for our car and that was weighing heavy on our hearts.

At this time our oldest son, Kelly, was not walking with the Lord and he had become "Job's comforter." He kept telling me I should go out and get a job. That particular evening I was beginning to agree with him. Were we just being presumptuous in thinking God would provide our needs?

I felt certain God had called me to minister to women and now Bill and I were also ministering to couples. We had seen much fruit, but financially it was not enough. I had been crying out to God. What were we to do? I felt we were in that "waiting room" of God and we definitely were building up our spiritual muscles, but we needed a huge breakthrough. I have heard it said that life always gets harder as we are about to approach the summit. Hopefully, we were about there—wherever "there" was.

Our pastor at that time had been very supportive of us and often I would go to the altar, or Bill and I both would go, and just pour out our hearts to God and weep before Him. Many times our pastor would come down, lay his hand on our back, and say, "Don't give up. Don't give up!" His encouragement was one thing that had kept us going as he felt God had definitely called us, but we were becoming quite discouraged as it seemed nothing was happening to prove this.

Sitting on the sofa and trying to tune out the voice of our son, I had gotten out my faithful journal and began to pen my thoughts. This was always a way for me to escape from the pressures. It felt like God had forgotten us. I knew He hadn't, but why was this so hard if we were in His will? Had we somehow veered from the path? So many questions and so few answers.

Tears began to roll down my cheeks. All the days and months of living by faith, trusting God for so many

> **It felt like God had forgotten us. I knew He hadn't, but why was this so hard if we were in His will? Had we somehow veered from the path?**

things, seemed to have taken its toll on me. I was weary from all this. The journey seemed much too long. As I was writing, I seemed to be writing my thoughts to God. "God, do You see where we are tonight? Do You care? Have we missed You?" I have since learned the greatest challenge in receiving great things from God is holding on to the last half hour. I remember a friend often told me what her father would say, "It's always too soon to give up."

I decided to call it a day and go to bed. Frankly, I just wanted to get alone and cry my heart out to God. Besides, it was getting late. It was almost 9:30 and I was about to get up when the doorbell rang. I couldn't believe it. Who could that be this time of night? By now I looked a wreck: mascara was running down my face, my shirt tail was out, and I certainly did not want to see anyone, much less have to talk to someone. I sent Kyle to the door. Bill was on the phone peeking around the corner, Kelly was looking curiously at this fellow that had just entered our home and wondering who he was and why he was calling at this late hour. Kayla was missing this mystery as she was still at work.

We had a long entrance area and I was trying to hear what was being said without anyone noticing me. We didn't have cordless phones at that time and Bill had stretched the cord almost out of shape in order to see who this mysterious visitor was. Kyle ran back into the den and said, "Mom, there is some guy here and he insists he needs to see you." At that point I knew there was no way to get out of this, so I reluctantly went to the door, but first I had to wipe the mascara from my eyes and try to look presentable.

This nice looking young man was standing in the foyer. I didn't pay a whole lot of attention to him as I was looking at this beautiful package he was holding, but if memory serves me correctly, he had dark hair and dark eyes. I immediately tried to gain composure and said to him, "Who are you and what is this?" Without blinking an eye he answered me and said, "I am not allowed to tell you but I was told to bring this to you."

Again, I asked him, "Who are you?" And again, this complete stranger said, "I was told to give this to you and now I must go." By now I was in sort of a daze as this seemed so bizarre. All I could muster up to say was, "Well, praise the Lord!" As he made his way to the door he turned and said, "Yes, praise the Lord." This stranger placed the package in my arms, opened the door, and left.

You can imagine my surprise. In fact, we were all shocked at what we had just experienced. Who was this fellow and what was in this box? And who sent him? It was all a big mystery! The boys were both looking in wonderment and yelling at me to open the package. The package was wrapped beautifully and elegantly. The paper was silver, the bows were silver and a peach color. There was a large peach colored rose attached to the package. It was almost too beautiful to unwrap, but of course curiosity was getting the best of all of us.

There was a card attached to the outside of the package. I decided to open the card before I tore into the box. Maybe that would explain this enigma. The card was a regular gift card and this verse was printed on the front of the card.

> *"When you're sad . . . I cry*
> *And when you hurt . . . I bleed*
> *I feel your pain*
> *And I know your thoughts*
> *So when all else crumbles to the ground*
> *I will stand as your support"*

Now, I opened the card up and someone had handwritten this note; on one side was this, *"For the times when I have doubted You, Lord, have mercy."* and on the other side of the page was this, *"Elaine, I care for your every need, no matter how minute they are. My word is the truth. I am working in your life and I will work things out. You can claim my promises. If I can deal with this small item, just think what I'm going to do for you. Love, Jesus."*

I'm sure by now you're already ahead of me in guessing what was in the box; yes, the forest green dress that I had longingly hung back on the rack and whispered in my heart, "Oh, Lord, I would love to have that." He saw

The Miracle of the Green Dress

and He heard. That day He saw me in that department store. Nothing escapes notice of our Heavenly Father. He cares for each of us watchfully and affectionately. He sees where I am at this very moment. He sees where you are at this moment. If a small, insignificant bird cannot fall from the sky without His awareness, how much more important we are to Almighty God.

Each time I tell this story my faith is boosted and I am encouraged at how aware God is of each of His children. May your faith be encouraged and may you realize He sees you right now at this very moment. You are never alone!

I had mentioned that we were in dire need of four tires for our car. A few days after Christmas, a money order came in the mail for $200. The remitter was signed "Jesus." We serve a God that is able to do *"Exceeding abundantly beyond all that we ask or think according to the power that works within us."* EPHESIANS 3:20

When I tell this story so many people ask if I know who sent it? Was it an angel? Only God knows those answers, but we do know an angel is a messenger of God and we also know God uses people to accomplish His work. Whoever, or whatever, it was a God thing and it was so timely!

LIVE EXPECTANTLY!

No Longer Will We Eat Manna

I distinctively remember the morning the Lord spoke to me and said, "No longer will you eat manna." I wasn't quite sure I knew what He meant, but remembering the story of the Israelites in Exodus when God first began to feed them manna they asked, *"What is it?"* (EXODUS 16:15). Later, I realized He was telling us that no longer would we be "fed" in a supernatural way. In other words, this living by faith was coming to an end. It had been eight years. The number eight in scripture means a new beginning.

So much had happened during these eight years of being spoon-fed by God. Though our income was not

> **"We never know how a single act of obedience can be the seed in another persons' life"**

great, God had definitely taken care of us in supernatural ways. But I longed for a time when we would once again have a regular income. I kept saying, "I want to live like normal people," whatever that meant.

I had become very involved in a women's ministry called Women's Aglow Fellowship. (Now known as

Aglow International) In fact, I had helped start the first Aglow chapter in our city. I must say, when I first was asked to serve on the board I was not interested, but thanks to my husband and his continuous urging for me to get involved, I did consent to serve on the board. For whatever reason, I just did not like women's meetings. I don't know why, but I tended to think women could get very snobbish in groups. Whether that was true or not, that was what I believed. Aglow was a non-profit organization and had started in Seattle, Washington. Four women had caught the vision for women coming together to worship the Lord, and from that small beginning many fellowships were starting up all over the United States as well as several overseas.

Several women came together in our city to start holding Aglow meetings. We held the meetings in the ballroom of a lovely hotel in our city. It seemed like women were coming out of the woodwork to attend. Sometimes we would have several hundred women in attendance. We would invite women from all around the United States to speak and many women were being touched. I always felt if you could reach the woman you could reach the home and that seemed proving to be true.

Although I had agreed to serve on this board, I can't say I was a very good board member. I didn't seem to have the vision for this and yet so many women were being touched. Bill had been invited to speak at a church that was in the northern part of our state. He would be speaking at two services so I traveled with him. There was a strong Aglow group in this area and many of the leaders attended the church where Bill was ministering.

Living Expectantly

We had gone out to lunch with some of these women and their husbands and during our conversation they asked if I was planning to attend the Aglow conference that was being held in Chicago. This was going to be an international conference and women from around the world would be attending.

I had received a brochure with the information telling about this conference, but I knew I could not attend because I did not have the money. I didn't bother to ask the Lord if He wanted me there, I just didn't feel I wanted to go. Anyway, when the women asked me if I was going to this gathering I said, "no." Then one of them was quite bold and said, "Have you prayed about this?" I have to tell you I had not prayed and I was quite embarrassed to tell them I hadn't. We dropped the subject and moved on to talk about something else. I felt relieved that I didn't have to explain why I was not going.

When we got back home I looked at my calendar to see if I had clear dates on the days of the conference. Amazingly enough, that entire week I had nothing on my calendar. That was rare as I was speaking quite often and rarely had an entire week with nothing scheduled. Later that morning one of the women from that Aglow group in the city where Bill had spoken called me on the telephone. I knew these women, but was not personally acquainted with any of them.

The woman that called was the president of the area board for that section of the state. She said, "Elaine, our board has prayed about this and we feel you are to go to that conference and we will pay for you to attend and cover all of your expenses." That got my attention!

I didn't know why I was to go, but by now I'm definitely sensing that this is a God thing, so I accepted their offer and started making plans to attend.

Being a woman, I immediately started thinking about what I would wear. I desperately needed a robe since I would be rooming with another person. My robe was not in the best of shape. Shortly after thinking about this, I got a phone call from a good friend. She was one of my closest friends, but we had never exchanged birthday gifts. I answered the phone and she immediately said, "Do you need a new robe?" Wow! This was becoming too much for my feeble mind. I'm not sure I had even prayed about a robe after thinking about needing one, and here is my friend asking me about a robe? This was without a doubt another God thing!

I told her everything that had taken place that morning; the phone call, my realizing I would be sharing a room with someone, and my concern about the shape of my old robe. I think she was as excited as me to realize she had definitely heard from God and He was telling her to buy me a robe. She gave me some money and I found the most beautiful robe that happened to be on sale and it was just what I wanted. I loved it. It had multi-colored stripes and I called it my "Joseph's robe of many colors." I continued to wear that robe until it was almost in shreds. It was a very special thing and a reminder of something I never wanted to forget. More than likely, the Aglow women that sent me to the conference, and my friend that bought me the robe, didn't realize how significant those things were for my destiny, and neither did I at the time We never know how a single act of obedience can be the seed of a miracle in another persons' life.

I attended the conference, still not that excited about this ministry for women, but why not go, my way was being paid. One evening they planned to have women from different nations share what was happening in Aglow in that particular nation. A woman from Romania got up to share. My heart was so stirred as she shared what she went through in order to bring God's word to hurting, and needy women! She lived behind barbed wire because the area was unsafe. In order to reach the women, she always carried a gun for safety and always prayed God's protection as she traveled. These women were coming to know Jesus because this woman was willing to risk her life to share the Good News! Need I tell you, something happened in my heart? I began to see the broader vision of what God was doing through this ministry for women and I knew I wanted to be involved. My heart's desire was to reach women for Christ and in time, God was going to give me a larger platform to do just that.

I had recently been selected as president of our local Aglow, and when I returned from that conference I could hardly wait to get up and share what God was doing

> **I could hardly wait to get up and share what God was doing around the world. I had caught the vision and I was on fire!**

around the world. I had caught the vision and I was on fire! God was really moving in our state and our area. We were able to start many fellowships. Women were finding that they had a place in ministry; not just working in the nursery or kitchen at their churches, but God was using them in places of leadership.

Eventually our area started expanding and I was asked to be president over an area. By now our state was divided into four sections, so that meant there were four area boards in Ohio. I had grown to love Aglow and all the ministry was doing to reach women. It was exciting. This was not a paid position as all the leaders were volunteers, but the benefits I received in doing this far exceeded any salary I might have gotten. I felt so privileged to be able to be part of this great work God was doing. God had given us a new car and I was more than willing to use it in the ministry. Traveling over a fairly large area to reach the section of the state over which I was in charge, I was putting a lot of miles on this car, but Bill and I both felt God wanted us to do this.

Bill and I were ministering to many couples, more and more doors were opening. I was being invited into several states now to share. We were excited. Our kids were growing up, Kyle had moved out on his own and was pursuing a career in art. He was an artist and had moved to Chicago as he wanted to make a name for himself. We had sold our big house and were renting as we had not found anything suitable for our needs at the time. Kelly was back in Texas attending Christ for the Nation Institute in Dallas. He had fallen in love with one of my best friend's granddaughter and they had married and were living in Dallas. Kayla was also married and two of our kids now had a child of their own

Living Expectantly

I had been invited to speak at an Aglow retreat in New York. When I got there and met all the leaders, I became terribly intimidated by these women. They were all well educated and most of them had attended Bible College so I felt very inadequate to be teaching anything to them. Believe me, I was struggling. BIG TIME! I went to bed that night and tossed and turned. I could not sleep. Fear was gripping my heart. I fell on my face and began to cry out to God. I said, "God, why have You allowed me to come to this group and minister? I have never done anything to open any door for myself. Why did You send me here?" It was not an audible voice I heard, but I knew that I knew it was Him speaking to me. In that quiet, firm voice I heard Him say to me. "I am preparing you for International."

I wasn't sure what that meant, but began to try and figure it out. I knew when He said "international" He was speaking about the Aglow headquarters. I thought perhaps He was telling me that at some point I would be asked to teach a workshop at one of the Aglow conferences. I could see myself doing that. In fact, from time to time other area leaders would hold workshops at a conference so I thought this was what He meant. This was in the month of June.

As I have mentioned, I have kept a journal for years. I did this as a young girl until my mother found my journal and read it. But once I became a Christian, I started keeping a journal regularly. It has really become a form of therapy for me as I write very personal things in it. In fact, not long ago, I decided I needed to write a disclaimer in the event that I died and family members started reading my writings. Let me share with you what I now write in the front of each journal.

"Writing my thoughts has become a catharsis for me. These writings are only a purging of my soul and not intended to bring blame, shame, hurt, or pain to others. They are only an expression of where I am in my journey to wholeness."

Another reason I enjoy journaling is because it is a source of reminder for me of all the things God has done. I have been thankful to have these journals to turn to as I have been writing this book. At times I get them out and re-read all the wonderful things God has done in our lives. It's sort of like "memorial stones." Remember in Joshua 4, Joshua told the twelve men he had appointed to take up a stone, and carry it across the water, and then place it there as a reminder of all God had done.

Once I got home, I immediately told Bill what God had said and wrote it in my journal, but I never breathed a word to anyone else. I thought, I will have a record of it in the event something does come about. In July, I received a call from the Women's Aglow International Office. The person calling had been appointed to serve on a selection committee as they were appointing new people to serve on the Corporate Board of Aglow. She was wanted to know if I was willing to have my name considered. I was shocked! How did they even get my name? At that time there were 150 or more Aglow Area Presidents in the United States. I had never even called the international office. I knew no one out there and no one knew me. I had met two women from the office at a leadership training conference but doubted if either of them would remember me.

As I already said, I was shocked! I was stunned. I came to my senses and asked her if I could pray about this before I would allow them to consider my name. I said I would like to pray about this for two weeks. She said there was no problem with me doing this. I also had asked her if this would mean I would have to move to Seattle and of course it would. But keep in mind, we did not own a house, our youngest son was out of our home at the time and we didn't have a job to hold us down. Was all this another God thing?

We told each of our children and asked them to pray and told both of our parents who were still alive at that time. We also called our pastor and asked if we could come in and talk with him. He immediately said, "Does this have to do with a move?" Did he know something we didn't know? Should I decide to have them consider me as a possible candidate and get selected, then our children had to be in agreement with this. It meant leaving them and our grandchildren. This was not going to be an easy thing to do. I had to know it was God!

We all prayed for the two weeks and at the end of this time we felt I should allow them to consider my name. At that time, the term was only for three years and at the end of three years they would evaluate the board member and see if they thought they should stay for another term. The person who was the Vice-president of the Foreign Fellowships Department had just finished her third year term so her name was up for consideration.

No Longer Will We Eat Manna

As VP of that particular department, she gave oversight to all the Aglow fellowships outside the United States. That certainly appealed to me as I definitely was ministry minded. I had not worked outside the home in seventeen years. I had been a stay at home wife/mother all the time my children were growing up. To go back into the work force was definitely a challenging thought. But we were laying it all before God and trying to find out what He was saying to us. This was not a small thing, it was huge! And keep in mind I had told the Lord over and over that I was more than willing to get a job, but at the same time I felt He had called me to minister to women. This looked like the perfect job!

Everyone was excited. Bill was ecstatic! He felt this was such a wonderful opportunity for me. My parents said they were so proud of me that I was even being considered. Our children were excited, but I had mixed emotions! Yes, it would be a wonderful opportunity, but could I do this? Was I usurping my husband's authority by taking such a position? I had so many questions. Why didn't God open the door for Bill? Why me?!? Times were much different back them. Few women were in any type of ministry. And of course, the hardest thing would be leaving our children and grandchildren.

At our recent Aglow retreat, our speaker had been a woman from Seattle. She was a powerful woman of God and a pastor. This was rare back then. I felt led to call her and ask her advice. She was extremely kind and helpful. I explained how I was worried about usurping Bill's authority. She asked me, "What does he think of this" and I told her he was encouraging me all the way.

And then she said to me, "If he approves this, then you are not out of order and don't box God in as to how He chooses to open doors." She also said I could trust God to close the door if this was not Him.

We talked with our pastor and he too was excited and not surprised. He had been sensing that change was coming and God was about to do something big for us. It had been a long journey, one we did not understand, but we were always trying to be obedient. And now we were going to see if this was what God had spoken to me about earlier when I felt He had said, "I am preparing you for international."

I still had not mentioned this to anyone outside our family other than our pastor. One morning I arrived at our Area board meeting. At that time our advisors met with us. We had three men that served as advisors and they were all pastors. When I got to the meeting two of them said, "I got a phone call from the international office asking about you." Of course the girls on the board heard this and they began to question me. I felt almost like I had betrayed them by not sharing what was happening, but on the other hand I felt I was to keep it private. They were each one very excited for me and not the least surprised. One of them said her son had told her recently that he thought I was going out to the international office to serve.

Later in the day while still at the board meeting, the international office called me. They told me the woman that was over the International Fellowship Dept. was going to stay in that position, but would I consider taking the position as Vice President of the Administration

Department? I had no idea what that job description would consist of, so I asked a few questions and it seemed like something I could do. I hesitated for a moment, prayed a very quick prayer, and said, "yes." Oh my golly, what had I done? Was I crazy or was I being led by His Spirit? I had such a gamut of emotions.

When I went back into the room with the board and advisors, I told them what had just happened and that it was not the position I had hoped it would be. One of the girls on the board quickly said, "You will not stay in that position forever! It will only be a door to something else." She said it with such a determined voice that I was sure she was right!

When I got home later in the day, the Aglow office called me once again to tell me I had been selected. Of course, this depended on the area boards voting and approving me. I didn't feel that would be a problem as things like that never had been. Once Bill and I talked about this and realized we would be moving and leaving our families and familiar routines, the reality of all this hit me full force. Could I do this? It seemed like such a price to pay, and yet, there was something within me thinking if I did not accept this I would always regret it and wonder what I had missed.

My pastor called the next day. He, too, had received a phone call from Aglow as they were checking my references. He said the church staff were all praying for us. I told him I was fearful. I questioned how this could be God when I was feeling such fear. I'll never forget his response. He said, "Elaine, sometimes doing the will of God can be very frightening." And then he said, "It will certainly be a stretching of your faith," but he felt in doing so we would come into another realm of faith with God. I was learning that peace does not always follow obedience! No wonder God always would preface, when sending His people out into something new, "Do not fear. Don't be afraid!" He knew and I was certain He understood all my apprehension!

Imagine. They were willing to hire me and didn't even know me. I flew out to Aglow and got acquainted with the people with whom I would be working. I wasn't going to start in this position until January so it was too early to find a place to live, but I did look at several places and got some ideas of where I would like to live. One of the secretaries who was also a Vice President, offered to look for a place for us and would send us all the information as she got it. She was extremely detailed and would send me much information with sketches and everything I needed, so I felt she would find us something.

When I got back from Seattle, Bill and I sat down and tried to estimate how much money we would need to make this trip and to get settled. Keep in mind, we are moving thousands of miles away and it would not be cheap. Aglow would give me a small allowance for the move, but not enough for everything that was needed for such a move. Having moved earlier to a smaller place, we had already downsized a lot, so that was helpful. At least that would make it less expensive to move all our things cross-country.

Several people asked me if we were taking all our things with us since my term was only for three years. What if I wasn't approved for another term? It was risky, but in reading the account of Abram when he was called, it said, *"And Abram took Sarai his wife and Lot his nephew, and all their possessions which they had accumulated."* That was my answer. I was going to take all my things with me. This would be our new home and only God knew for how long, but I wanted our things with us. We find this account in Genesis 12:5. I could identify with Abram. He was going to a land he knew nothing about, but God called and he obeyed. My biggest question was how the money would be provided for us to make this huge transition?

When word got out that I was moving to Seattle where I would be serving as a Vice president on the Women's Aglow Fellowship International Board, I began to hear from many Aglow women and how excited they were for me. That made me very happy. I think they felt I was like an ambassador going to another state in order to represent them, and in a sense that was exactly what I would be doing. When I would go out to speak, it became the norm for someone, or maybe several, to come up and hand me a check or money and tell me they wanted to help send me out there. The love that was being demonstrated to me was overwhelming.

I spoke at one church during this time and shared my story of finally getting our bare bedroom decorated and all that God had done to bring this about. Afterward a woman came up to me and said, "God told me to give you this to buy your ginger jar lamp." She handed me a very generous check. It had taken awhile for that entire prayer to be answered, but God answered. I continued to be amazed at His provision—over and over and over again.

As I had learned to do so many times in the past, I started making a list of what I felt we needed in our new house. As always, I was not trying to be extravagant, but practical, but I wanted to cover all this in prayer. Once I got the list completed, I prayed over it and stuck it in my Bible and waited expectantly to see how God would answer this prayer. I was feeling both excitement and fear. Excited about this opportunity, but fearful about the unknown. This was definitely an unknown thing for us. Like Peter, I felt we were stepping out on the water and like Peter, I knew we had to keep our eyes on Jesus or we too might sink!

Once I had been approved by the area officers in the field, I received congratulatory notes from some of the Vice Presidents in the international office with whom I

> **I was feeling both excitement and fear. Excited about this opportunity, but fearful about the unknown.**

would soon be working. Their notes were very encouraging. One note in particular touched my heart deeply. I want to share with you. She said, "Elaine, I was on the selection committee, and just felt a leaping in my spirit when we chose you. The funny part is, I don't have a face to put your name with, or even a voice, as I don't believe we've ever talked that much by phone, so I know it was the Spirit of God bearing witness." That helped me so much as I was still struggling with that age old question; "had I heard from God?" Little did I know what a wonderful friend this woman would become. We even have the same birthday and she never fails to remind me that I am the oldest, but I keep reminding her I am the prettiest! Only kidding, of course! After all these years we still talk fairly often on the phone and have even been able to visit each other since I left Seattle.

A woman that I did not know well, but knew of through a mutual friend, sent me an encouraging word. She had left the familiarity of her home and moved to Germany where she continues to reside and is in ministry. If anyone could understand my emotions I felt this woman surely would. "I do pray God's richest blessings for you in the days ahead. To my present knowledge, anyone in the scriptures who made a great move (even geographically) for God was greatly blessed. I personally believe we take giant steps forward in God when we're willing to leave family and friends to answer His call. And not only do we take steps forward, but Jesus said, 'everyone that hath forsaken houses or brethren for My name's sake, shall receive a hundredfold, and shall inherit everlasting life.' He also said, 'If any man serve Me, him will my Father honor.' So, you've got a lot going for you already!"

Another encouraging word came that spoke directly to my heart. "Do not allow the comforts of today rob you of the service of tomorrow. Neither should you allow the fears of tomorrow rob you of God's will for your life today. Do not settle down now. Pack your bag, take your purse in your hand, and go forward. Behold, I have set the land before you. Possess it! Let the people know that I love them enough to send you to them with a message

Living Expectantly

from me. Be not weary in well-doing, for in due season you shall reap if you faint not."

You're probably thinking with all the doubts I have had about this calling that I am like Thomas who was known in the scriptures as "Doubting Thomas." You remember how he said he would only believe when he could see? Well, I was not seeing anything, but I was moving forward and totally trusting God in this, but my flesh does get afraid. Jesus was so good to Thomas and, I believe very understanding of him in that place and He reached out and showed Thomas the nail-scarred hands. You see, Thomas was soon stepping out into an unknown place, going to India as a missionary. He needed that encouragement, and I needed those notes and letters and words of encouragement too. It's an unknown future for us, but we know Who holds our future in His hand!

Seattle, Here We Come

The movers had packed all of our things. We were ready to start this journey and set out for the city of Seattle. It was the third day of December. We thought by leaving in early December we would miss a lot of bad weather. That was very naïve on our part. Little did we know we would be driving right into many storms, both physical and spiritual. As we drove out of the driveway and said "good-bye" to family, I almost lost it. I was convulsing with tears. Bill kept saying, "Honey, we don't have to do this." And he was right, we didn't. But would I miss the call of God if I chose to stay in the familiar? We continued to press forward!

In Hebrews 13:13 it reads, *"Let us go out to Him, outside the camp."* I was reminded that there are times that God will call us to live outside the tent, outside that which is normal, and predictable. When this happens, we must leave the world of our senses, abide in the world of our spirit, and remind ourselves that the greatest thing is to seek God and to know Him and His ways. This again, is kingdom living!

We had spoken at our church a couple of nights before we left. God gave us a good word to share and afterward they surprised us with a lovely farewell party. We felt so loved and honored. They even presented us with a generous financial gift. That gift, combined with all the other gifts we had received, gave us more than the amount we asked of God. We were learning that God is "the God of much more."

The farther we drove toward our destination, the worse the weather became. Unfortunately, we weren't able to make good time due to lack of visibility much of the time. The ice and snow were horrendous in many places. Normally we tried to find a place to stay before night came, but one evening we took a chance and kept going trying to make better time. That was a mistake! At some point we hit black ice. In case you don't know what that is, you have no indication of ice in the area until you start sliding. It is invisible to the eye. That is what is known as "black ice."

We went into a slide and ended up in a ditch. We knew there was no way we would be able to get ourselves out of this predicament. What were we to do? It was late, dark, icy, and not too many vehicles on the road at that time of night. Now thinking back, I would imagine Father God who *"sits in the heavens and laughs"* (PSALM 2:4) was sitting up there and said to those around Him, "What an opportunity for Me to show myself strong on their behalf." Out of nowhere came a truck with two men in it. They did not speak a word to us, but jumped out of the truck and pushed our vehicle back onto the highway, then left without a word. Angels? Probably! But whoever or whatever they were, God sent them!

Do I need I tell you how grateful we were? We just

couldn't stop praising God for His goodness. Shortly after that we found a little motel. It wasn't much to look at and normally we would not have chosen it, but we knew we needed to get off the road and we were able to get a room and settled in for the night still thanking God for being *"A very present help in trouble."* PSALM 46: 1B

I was still grieving and crying over leaving our loved ones behind. Kelly and Kimberly were living in Texas, Kayla and Mark were in Ohio, and Kyle was alone in Chicago. I was especially grieving for him being alone. Even though we didn't see him as often, being in Ohio we were much closer to him than we would soon be in Seattle. There again, it was another trust issue. Could we trust God with our children? Or, better still, would we trust Him with our children? The farther we drove the more distance it seemed we were putting between us. The ultimate test of faith for a parent is giving our children back to Him, which was what we were trying to do.

After five days of driving in the worst weather conditions we had ever seen, we arrived at our new little home. While in Seattle at the time of the interview, I had looked at these condos but it was too soon to secure one, plus

Bill and I had started praying that God would open the door for us to live in this area and here we were in the home God Himself had made possible.

they didn't even have one available. But the area seemed to be perfect for our needs and was close to the office, so after returning to Ohio, Bill and I had started praying

Seattle, Here We Come

that God would open the door for us to live in this area and here we were in the home God Himself had made possible.

While driving to Seattle, we saw several moving vans from the company that was carrying our furniture that were turned over or stuck in ice. We prayed none of them contained our things. We had carried a few things with us so we could manage until our moving van arrived. We also planned to buy a mattress, so we went out and got one that same day, and it would be delivered the next day. In the meantime, we spent the night with one of the women that worked at the office.

As grateful as we were to have this nice place as our home, when I walked in and saw the carpet it was BAD, AWFUL! ATROCIOUS! Having a very sensitive eye toward color and my surroundings, I thought to myself, "Oh, God, I thought you brought us out here to bless us. This is horrible!" My mood changed from gratefulness to anger. I hate to admit this, but that's where I was. I was thinking, "How can I live with this?" And there was nothing we could do but make the best of what I thought was a bad situation.

We needed to eat, so we piled back in the car and found a fast food place to grab a bite. I was so glad no one knew me in this place because I did not have a very happy face on at that time. I was in a foul mood. Bill was trying to tell me everything was going to be okay, but it sure was not helping. While sitting there, I began to talk to the Lord under my breath. I was already asking Him to forgive me for my ungrateful attitude. I remember saying to Him, "Lord, You're the God of the impossible.

You are the great interior decorator. I don't know how You will do this, but I know You can help me decorate in such a way no one will even notice that carpet." And I was very sincere. I knew in my heart He could help me do something to manage what seemed, at that moment, like an insurmountable problem. I gave it to Him and honestly was resting in this. It would be okay.

Someone had brought us some folding chairs, so we had a mattress, two folding chairs, and a cardboard box that we used as a table. We were settled in to wait for the movers to bring our furniture. We found out that they were in Oregon and they were safe, but due to the horrific storms they were stuck on a mountain so it would still be several days before our things arrived. They could not risk trying to get that large, heavy van down a mountain until some of the ice melted or was removed. So we waited as patiently as we knew how.

One night we were sitting in the living room and I noticed a place on the carpet that looked like a circle had been cut out, but the carpet was still there. I went over to examine it and sure enough you could pick the carpet piece up and run your hand under the mat. I called the landlord to make her aware of this in the event she might think we had done something. She told us she would send a carpet man out to inspect the problem. Sure enough he did come out and the landlord called us back quite apologetic. She said, "I am so sorry, but he feels we need to replace the carpet. I know this might be an inconvenience, but we will go ahead and do this as well as replace the carpet throughout the house. Would you like to go with me and pick out the carpet?" Would

I?!? One of the things I had written on my list that I hoped to get was neutral color carpeting. Well, guess what? I got to pick out neutral color carpeting that went throughout the house. It's amazing what can happen when our attitude changes! I can still hear our son Kelly saying to his children when they were younger, "I think someone needs an attitude adjustment." And so often, that little one would put on a happy face or get a more loving attitude. As believers we need to be reminded of that from time to time ourselves. Our attitudes can be a real indication of what is going on in our heart. And God is always after our heart! Only you can choose your attitude. No one can choose it for you.

I was dreading Christmas. Holidays have such a way of bringing back memories and I was prepared to think we would have a very unpleasant Christmas since we would be away from our family. Strangely I awoke on December 23rd, two days before the big day, and I can't explain what had happened, but I felt I had turned a corner, the struggle was over. I felt I had the victory. How could that be when we were here and they were there? It was definitely a God thing. I felt as if I was seeing with new eyes; eyes of excitement and hopefulness. We made it through the holiday and actually felt quite content. We had bought and decorated a small tree. I'm not sure what we ate that day, but we put music on the record player, turned on the gas logs, and sat and admired our pretty little home. We thanked God for bringing us to this place. Suddenly we were living expectantly for what God had in store for us.

As we thought about all this and what had been

Living Expectantly

taking place since I had that word back in June, it was nothing short of miraculous. The living by faith, eating the "manna" was over. I now had a job and would be doing something that I loved, working with women and getting paid to do it. Thank You, Jesus! Now it was beginning to make sense to us that the last eight years did have purpose. God had heard our prayers and we were about to embark on a new adventure, in a new place—a place of promise.

We had walked through the fires, the storms, the wilderness, but we felt we had now entered, what seemed to be, the promise land. I was reminded of that scripture in Deuteronomy 8—my life line for those eight years. I went back and re-read verse 7, *"For the Lord your God is bringing you into a good land, a land of brooks of water, of fountains and springs, flowing forth in valleys and hills"* and as you keep reading verses 8, *"a land where you will eat without scarcity, in which you shall not lack anything."* Yes, it had been hard. Would I want to walk that way again? No, but at the same time I learned so much about the faithfulness of God that I probably never would have learned otherwise. He is good, He is faithful and you can count on His promises. Where you are now may not seem like He is even with you. But I believe one day you can look back and see how He was always with you and see His hand leading you even though you did not know it. *LIVE EXPECTANTLY!!*

It's Off to Work I Go

Because the Aglow office closed during the Christmas holidays, I had several days to get our home in order. We were already settling in and it truly felt like home. The carpet had been laid, our furniture had arrived safely, and we were now getting acquainted with the area. We located the different grocery stores, the mall, the Aglow office, and were eager to find a church. We had only met one couple but had talked on the phone to my boss and a few more of the women from the office. Everyone seemed so nice. I was getting excited to start my new job, but also apprehensive. Would they like me? Would I like them? Would I fit in? Could I do the job? Would I only be there for three years and then turned away after my first term? I had so many questions and so few answers at the moment.

At that time, the office was housed in an old elementary school. It was charming the way these women had turned that old building into such an attractive place. It was easy to see the touches that only a woman could bring. Since Aglow was formed as a ministry to women, we only had women as employees. We were not sexist in any way, but at that time it seemed the right thing

It's Off to Work I Go

to only employ women. At this writing, men have now been welcomed into Aglow as members and could be employed there as well.

My office was located in the space where the school nurse once had her office and I had a private room along with an adult size bathroom. That was a real bonus considering the main bathroom had small stalls with tiny, low setting toilets and sinks. Keep in mind, this had been a school for kindergarten and elementary students.

I was allowed to decorate my office to suit my personality, and it was in dire need of being painted. Already I was thinking of how I could get this done since there was nothing in my Aglow budget to provide for it, but I had been learning that God has a way where there is none.

We had about 40 or 50 employees at that time. Through the years we were able to reduce that number significantly once we each had personal computers. I was serving as Vice-President of the Operations Dept. I believe we had about 15 or 16 women in our department alone. Under the Operations Department was the Human Resource Dept., Shipping, Print Shop, and oversight for the mainframe computer. Our department was also responsible to work with the school district to maintain the lease and the upkeep for the building. To say I was overwhelmed was an understatement! What had I gotten myself into? I understood Job when he said, "I curse the day I was born." I was cursing the day I had said "yes" to accepting this position! Lord, help!! Actually that is an exaggeration, but I was nervous.

Remember the story of Gideon? His story is found in Judges 6. He was beating out wheat in the wine press when an angel of the Lord appeared to him. I would imagine Gideon was a little startled by this visitor. And then the visitor addressed him by saying, "The Lord is with you, O valiant warrior." Although the scripture doesn't say this, I would think Gideon was looking around wondering if this angel of the Lord was at the right house. "Me, a valiant warrior? Surely he has the wrong person and address." Think of Simon, later known as Peter. When he met Jesus, everything began to change. One day he was weak and cowardly denying he knew Jesus, another day he was courageous in his faith in Jesus.

In Matthew 16:18, we see Jesus calling him Peter which meant "rock." And Jesus was appointing Peter as the fearless leader of the infant church of Jerusalem. It's not about who we are, but Whose we are. When we make ourselves available to Jesus, watch what He does. And here I am at this wonderful ministry for women and God has called me a "Vice-President." I was to learn that my sufficiency was not in me, but in Him who had called me. One morning while in prayer I felt God said, "I have prepared you spiritually and now I will groom you formally."

More than likely you have heard this story, but it seems to be such a good illustration of what I am saying. There was a sculptor working on a large piece of marble. He had an instrument in his hand and was chipping away at the marble. A little girl happened to see the sculptor doing this and stood watching him for sometime. At the moment, she had no idea what he was doing, but later the child came back to where the sculptor was working and she saw a beautiful lion. The little girl said, "Wow! How did you know there was a lion inside that ugly piece of rock?" You see, God doesn't see us as we are, but how He created us.

Someone took me around to each office and introduced me to the other women. I found each person to be warm, friendly, and accepting. Already I was feeling connected and part of what God was wanting to do through this ministry. At times I felt I should pinch myself to see if this was really happening. As I thought back on how all this came about—me a total unknown being selected to serve in this capacity—it was surreal. Only God could have orchestrated such an amazing thing!

As I started settling in, I was aware of how much there was to learn. Many of the women had been with the Aglow office since the inception of the ministry. They had learned everything from the ground up. Aglow actually started in 1967 and their "office" was in a small home garage. As the ministry grew, they outgrew the garage and eventually moved to the school building. I felt like such a novice. Having not worked outside my home for seventeen years I struggled very much with feelings of inadequacy. Often I would even question if I had been led by the Lord to accept this position. It was a battle of the mind. Everything starts with our thinking and we can think ourselves into wrong beliefs.

I became discouraged and continued to question my decision to move to Seattle and take this position. Over and over I kept asking God if I had made a mistake. One particular day, after pouring over what seemed like reams of paper trying to learn all there was to learn, I was wiped out. It was a huge stretch and I was doubting my call

Living Expectantly

and also afraid that they—my boss and the other Vice-Presidents—were sorry they had hired me. Oh, how our mind can play such tricks on us and cause us to believe these lies, but at that time it all seemed true!

When I got home, I told Bill all I was feeling. He was very sympathetic with me and tried to help me to see that this was all a lie, just an attack from the enemy, but it felt so real! I went to bed that night feeling totally defeated—a failure—and now if this didn't work out we would have to go back to Columbus and I would have to admit defeat. I tossed and turned all night. I was so restless. I awoke and looked at the bedside clock and it was exactly 1:35 am. I don't believe I closed my eyes after that, but laid there in fear. I cried out, "God, have I missed You? Did I make a mistake?"

I dragged myself into the office the next morning. Having not slept the night before, I was already exhausted and feeling defeated. What was I to do? When I arrived home later that day, I discovered a friend from back home had sent me a note. I was a little upset to see such a small envelope as I had been hoping she would write me a long, newsy letter, but I could tell that was impossible because of the size of the note, but whatever size, I was thankful to hear from my friend. I hurriedly ripped it open and here is what she had written . . .

"Dear Sister,

Today, Thursday, Dec. 27th at 4:35 am I awakened and the Lord laid you on my heart. I began to pray and intercede for you and in the Spirit I saw you

It's Off to Work I Go

crying and saying, 'Lord, have I made a mistake?' No, dear Sister, you have not made a mistake, nor have you missed the Lord, you are in a time of transition and that is a very hard place to be and when you settle down and set your hand to the plow and do not look back, the Lord will begin to move and open doors in a mighty way. He has given you great responsibility because He knows you can handle it and you are very thorough in what you do, but you must stop the weeping and crying and set your hand to the plow."

Now keep in mind, this was so miraculous! My friend had been awakened at 4:35 am and even though I did not receive the letter on that same day, God awoke us at the same hour even though there is a three-hour time difference. And then, think of this: she wrote the note before the event had even happened! On Dec. 27th, the Aglow office was still closed and I had not even started to work. It was several days later when I had actually started to work that the note reached me. But the same day the note arrived I had awakened at 1:35 am crying out to God, "have I missed You, have I made a mistake?" The same words she had already heard in the Spirit.

This was HUGE! This was God! It was a lifeline for me to hold on to in the days ahead. Imagine what a word of encouragement that was for me. And then Holy Spirit reminded me of this scripture, *"It will also come to pass that before they call, I will answer."* (ISAIAH 65:24). Before I had even cried out to God, He was sending me that word of encouragement. As I think about this I am so thankful that my friend was obedient and sent me that note. How often do we get something from God and fail to pass it on? Obedience, even in what might seem unimportant in our mind, could be the difference in another person's life. Follow through and watch what God will do.

While I was the V.P. of Operations, it was always a stretch. Eventually I did learn to trust that I was exactly where God wanted me and even though I didn't always feel like it, I came to know I had been chosen by God for that job at that time in my life. *"And He said to me, My grace is sufficient for you, for power is perfected in weakness."* When we rely on our own strength it actually becomes weakness, but weakness that knows itself to be weakness is actually strength. Every element of self-reliance has to be put to death by God. It seems like an oxymoron to say that, but there again, that is kingdom living, the opposite of what the world teaches. (II CORINTHIANS 12:9)

Bill and I settled into a very nice church and filled out a questionnaire regarding who we were and what our giftings were. It wasn't long before two men knocked on our door. They were out meeting people that had visited

> **When we rely on our own strength it actually becomes weakness, but weakness that knows itself to be weakness is actually strength.**

their church. We got acquainted, told them some of the things we had done while in Ohio, and eventually we were invited to take over a young adult class. We didn't stay in that role very long as we realized we were much better with married couples than singles. But during that time God placed a young man in our life that was part of this group. He happened to be a painter by trade and wanted to do something for us. I asked if he would paint my office. He and another fellow were more than willing.

The color peach was very popular then so I chose a nice shade of peach to paint my office. I should say it looked like a very nice shade on the color chart, but I would soon learn that colors on the chart and colors in the room could be quite different. Bill and I had gone to Canada to speak that same weekend these guys had arranged to paint. The entire time we were gone, I couldn't help but think about getting back and seeing the results. I was so excited that it was finally going to be painted.

Well, I was in for quite a surprise! Not only did they paint the walls, but they painted the ceiling and believe me that shade of peach was nothing like what I had expected from looking at the chart. I had to live with that bright color the entire time we were in that school building. If anyone came to the office to see me, the girl at the desk would point the direction of my room and then tell them, "It's the peach colored room." That color radiated even out into the hall. I got a lot of teasing about my choice of colors, but I was finally able to laugh about it myself!

I stayed in that position for eight years. Although it was a wonderful experience for me and I learned quite a bit about administration, I felt I was drying up spiritually. I knew I had a call on my life to minister to women; that was my niche. I came alive when I was able to bring hope and expectancy to women and though I had been speaking a lot in the field of Aglow and had traveled to a few places outside the United States, something was missing. I kept crying out to God. I didn't want to leave Aglow, but at the same time I felt I was born for something besides sitting behind a desk. I eventually talked to Jane, our President, and bared my heart to her. She encouraged me to stick it out and not quit. At that time many changes were being made in the different offices and positions and I was hopeful that another door would open for me, or another position would be created, but I had no idea what it might be.

If you recall, when I was first asked about my name being considered for a position in the International Office of Aglow, I was told that the position being considered was for the International Fellowship office. At that time, they approved the Vice-President of that department for another term so that was a closed door. Then they asked if I would be willing to serve as Vice-President of Administration? (That name was eventually changed to Operations Dept.) I quickly prayed under my breath and felt I should accept the offer. When I went back to the meeting with the girls on the Aglow Area Board one of the officers said to me, "You will not stay in that position forever, but it will only be a door to something else." The number eight means, "new beginning." Was God about to open a new door of opportunity, a new beginning? Then I learned that the Vice-President of International Fellowship had decided to resign and go back to her home in Oklahoma. I'm not sure how long she had been in that position, but she felt it was time for a change.

I started praying, and praying hard. I knew that would be a place where I could really thrive. In that position, I would give oversight to the women of other nations. It would be a more "hands on" position with the leadership—training them, encouraging them, starting fellowships within new nations. I remember the day Jane and her assistant called me to their office. My heart was beating very fast! Were they going to offer this position to me, or did they have something else in mind? Honestly, I was afraid I would have a heart attack before they got to the reason of why they wanted to speak to me. I was certain my heart would beat out of my chest and then they finally got around to why I was there. Jane asked me how I would feel about moving into that department? Need I tell you my answer? It was "YES! YES! YES!"

I have learned God is never early and never late about answering our prayers. It must be according to His timetable, not ours, and I know from experience, that waiting is not easy, but He never wastes our time. There is a time of preparation and once we are thrust into that place we can know He has prepared us for what is ahead. I love something former Arkansas Governor, Mike Huckabee, said, "The preparation is more important than the presentation." And we know from studying the Scriptures that God always prepared His leaders.

My Heart Has Been Enlarged for the Nations

Once I moved into this new department—new to me—I had a lot to learn. I needed to learn many different nations, where they were located, etc., and get acquainted with the leadership within each nation. Unfortunately I don't recall how many nations Aglow was in at that time, but I'm sure it was around 120 or more. This ministry was making such an impact on nations around the world and today it still is.

At the time God raised up Aglow, there were few things for women to do when it came to Christian work. In the churches, a woman was welcome to teach children, work in the kitchen, and have little gatherings for women, but reading Genesis 1:27 we see an unfolding of God's plan *"And God created man in His own image, in the image of God He created him; male and female He created them."* In verse 28 we see God enforcing this point again, *"And God blessed them and said to them, 'Be fruitful and multiply and fill the earth, and subdue it; have dominion over the fish of the sea, over the birds of the air, and over every living thing that moves on the earth."*

Everything that God created was excellent in His sight. Neither the man nor the woman was made more than the other in the image of God. Human beings are at the very pinnacle of all that God created and the relationship between male and female is the very foundation from which God has intended to accomplish His work upon this earth. God never intended for the woman to be a second-rate person, nor did He intend for the woman to be superior to the man. He created them! And only in working together will the Church fulfill God's plan.

In the book of Exodus we see a woman that God used in a specific way. Her name was Miriam, the sister of Aaron and Moses. She was the oldest of the siblings and in Exodus 15:20–21 we see that she was referred to as a prophet or prophetess. Miriam loved the Lord and she was a leader and model to the Israeli women. After crossing the Red Sea, we see Miriam proclaimed and sang of the power and faithfulness of God! She danced before the Lord and played her tambourine. She was a worshipper. Unfortunately, she was quick to criticize and became quite critical of her brother, Moses, when he married a dark-skinned woman from Ethiopia. Miriam despised this woman not because of her color, but because she was a foreigner. And knowing how women can be, perhaps Miriam was jealous of this woman since Miriam was getting up in years.

Whatever Miriam did, it caused God's anger to rise up. Aaron also spoke against his brother because of the woman, but it was Miriam that was punished. Scripture isn't clear why Aaron was not punished, but it would seem from the order of the names in Scripture that Miriam was the instigator and possibly influenced her brother. At one time Miriam had been a picture of unity among the people, but she became critical and stirred up discord and disunity.

Numbers 12: 9–16 tells us that *"the anger of the Lord burned against <u>them</u> and God departed."* The cloud of Gods' presence was withdrawn from over the tent and Miriam was leprous! When someone came near a person with leprosy, the person was to cry out, "Unclean, Unclean!" Think how humiliating that must have been for Miriam. Thankfully her younger brother, Moses, had a forgiving heart and immediately began to cry out to God to heal his sister! She had to bear that shame for seven days outside the camp and Scripture tells us, *"And the people (the Church) did not move on until Miriam was received again."*

Personally speaking, I believe this is a prophetic picture of women. It is as if women had been lepers and had to be cast aside, but until women were restored to the right place that God intended; side by side with the man—the Church could not move forward. She had to be received! And I believe Aglow was raised up for that purpose, to show women they had a place where they would be accepted to minister. As a result of this ministry, women around the world have found a place where they can use their talents and gifts to reach others for the Kingdom of God.

I will always be grateful for the Aglow ministry. I never thought of myself as being a leader; I never realized I had any gifts or talents that could bring glory to God until I became involved with the Aglow ministry. When I first began as a volunteer in Aglow, I was very shy about speaking or doing anything publicly. To speak in public was a terrifying experience for me and nothing could have been harder for me, than praying out loud. Through this ministry I learned that God could use someone like me, and with Him by my side I began to evolve into the person He had created me to be. There was a "lion" (or lioness) inside of me just waiting to be brought forth! I had a "roar," a voice, and God was wanting me to express it! Today Aglow is in over 165 nations and on 6 continents. That is incredible! Women from all walks of

> **Women from all walks of life, all ages, all cultures, are discovering that they, too, have something God wants to use to reach others.**

life, all ages, all cultures, are discovering that they, too, have something God wants to use to reach others. Aglow has grown into a world wide movement reaching over 17 million people annually and now men can be members of Aglow.

God had opened a door for me to travel around the world and minister to women! Need I tell you how excited I was?!? I had traveled a few times overseas, but now I would be in charge of setting up the trips and deciding where to go. I was eager to visit Africa. At that time there was a lot going on, and I wanted to get better acquainted with the leadership. I had planned to go alone but one of our prayer coordinators asked if she could travel with me.

That worked out much better than me traveling alone to so many nations. We planned to connect in New York and travel to Rome and then several African nations.

I've forgotten now how long we were away, but it was not a short trip because we were visiting seven or eight nations. I definitely wanted to be well prepared for this trip, so I went out and bought a huge suitcase. When I say "huge," believe me, it was HUGE! That was my first mistake. People had warned me about drinking the water while in third world nations, eating the food, and on and on and on, so, I bought a water purifier to carry along. I took a lot of different snacks and that type of thing. I was well prepared as far as what I took with me, but what I had not prepared for was how I was going to lug all this baggage around!

After moving to Seattle and joining Aglow, I realized how essential it was for me to have intercessors. I needed women that would be committed to pray for me. I knew I was on the frontline now, and therefore the enemy would want to attack me in anyway he could. I began to pray that God would raise up intercessors for me. I believe it was at my first conference as a member of the board when a woman from Pennsylvania felt God laid me on her heart to begin praying for me. At some point she called the office and shared that with me. I was thrilled. God had answered my prayer. Eventually this woman pulled together several more women from her area and they all took me on as someone to cover in prayer. Not only did this woman become my personal intercessor, but also a good friend that traveled with me many times.

When she heard I was going on my first outreach trip, she sent me a lovely leather wallet that was large enough to carry my passport, itinerary, charge cards, etc., in one place. She even had my initials engraved in gold on this beautiful black leather wallet. It looked imposing! It looked like something a VP would carry with them. I was impressed!

But I have to tell you, there was one small problem I had not thought about. It did not fit in my purse. I had to carry it along with my purse. No problem, right? Stay tuned you will see!

On this first trip, parts of Africa were having a fall-like season so I needed a light wrap. I purchased a darling sweater at Seattle's best store, Nordstrom.. I had purchased a little carrier on wheels so I could place my carry on luggage on it. I attached this darling sweater on the carrier as well. While going through the airport in New York to connect with my friend, someone stole this darling little sweater! I should have been suspicious that things might get worse before they got better. Trying to be a good sport and keeping my attitude right, I tried to not get upset and told myself I could always find another sweater in South Africa.

Our first stop was in Rome and from there we were to depart the next morning for Egypt. Several people had warned me to be extremely careful while in the Rome airport as it was known for people trying to steal purses and passports. When our plane arrived in Rome, my luggage was not there. The personnel assured me it would arrive on the next plane early the next morning. We checked in to our hotel, freshened up a little and then took a taxi to shop for a few things that I would need before I got my luggage. We also did a little sightseeing, went back to our hotel and went to bed. We had a very busy day ahead of us.

I awoke quite early the next morning and immediately called the airlines to check on my luggage. "Yes," they told me, "your luggage had arrived and you can pick it up before departing for Egypt." We rushed to get to the airport in plenty of time so I could pick up my things. In all my years of traveling, I had never, ever put my teaching notes in my checked baggage, but for some reason, this time I had. God is the only One that knows why and He was probably shaking His head wondering Himself why I did that. My friend stayed upstairs while I went down into the place where my luggage was being stored. I have never seen so much luggage! Mounds and mounds of suitcases everyplace! I took my receipts to the proper department and they agreed: according to the paper work my luggage was there, but there was a problem . . . they didn't know where!

As I have already mentioned, we were leaving this airport and flying to Egypt. We had a very tight schedule and because we were going to so many nations, we had to make each connection at the time they were scheduled. At that time, flights to Egypt only flew out of Rome a couple of days a week and if we didn't make this connection we would be staying in Rome for a few more days.

When the attendant could not find my luggage, I attempted to look for it on my own. Remember, there were tons of luggage throughout the area. I was walking as fast as I knew how, praying as hard and furious as I knew how, binding up the enemy, telling him he could not hold my luggage back. I was talking out loud, so I'm sure people thought I might be a little deranged in my head. To tell you the truth, at that time I was! Finally, I spotted that enormous suitcase and my teaching notes. I threw my things in a cart and made my way back up to where my traveling companion was waiting for me. For some reason, the wheels on this particular cart would not move so I had to take my things out and switch carts.

Remember, I was still wearing the clothes I had started out in when I left Seattle the day before. I had dressed so carefully. I thought I looked really stylish! I had a cute two piece ensemble that I had purposely purchased for traveling; a split skirt (remember when those were in?), a jacket that matched, and a silk blouse. Well, I was getting a little nervous because of the time factor and rushing as quickly as I could. I got in line to get my seat assignment, and gave them my ticket only to discover I did not have the darling, black leather wallet with the gold initials engraved on the outside. By now I was not looking or feeling like a VP. I was petrified! And I knew what I had done. In the rush of having to get another cart, I had left that wallet in the first cart. My friend screamed at me, "Well, go find it!" I quickly obeyed and rushed to the area where I had been earlier.

Have you ever tried finding a needle in a haystack? That was the dilemma. There were hundreds of carts all around the area where I had been and I could not find the one I had left behind. My heart was beating out of my chest. I was no longer perspiring, I was past that stage. I was sweating like a boar hog. I don't really know what that means, just ask another Texan. But I do know this, it was a lot! It was running from under my armpits down into my waist. I have a lot of hair, but it is very fine. By now my bangs were practically in my eyes, and my hair was hanging in my face from sweat!

My mind had gone crazy. I was thinking of what I would tell my office. Keep in mind, this was my first outreach trip on my own and I was sure it would be my last! Not only did I have my own money and credit cards, but I also had a credit card from Aglow and a lot of cash they had given me in the event I was not able to use a card. And of course, no passport. I might not ever even get back to Seattle! I went inside an office to report the loss. They questioned me; had I made a copy of my passport to carry somewhere other than that wallet? Duh! I had never thought of that. No! I was scared, embarrassed and my friend was staring holes in me. I could tell she was angry. I told her to go on alone and we would connect later, but she was not budging! Then a "suddenly" of God happened. A man walked into the office and said, "Is Elaine Keith in here?" I turned around and he handed me my beautiful black leather wallet with the engraved gold initials and said, "Be careful in the future!"

Oh, if I had time I would have hugged that man and all the people in that room. My grateful cup was running over. God had rescued me! I just wanted to start praising and worshipping Him, but we were about to miss our flight. We got on the plane and I immediately rushed into the bathroom, sat down on the toilet seat, lifted my hands up to God, and wept and praised Him for what He had done! And then I looked in the mirror and almost screamed out loud! My face was beet red. My hair was hanging in my face. My blouse was dripping wet. But I had my beautiful black leather wallet with the gold initials engraved on the front and once I could clean up I might look like that VP again

World, Here We Come

After what happened in Rome, I was hoping and praying the rest of the trip would be a breeze. I later asked the Lord what that was all about, my losing my passport and everything. I felt He dropped this in my heart; "Elaine, you will be going into many nations, many unexplored territories, doing things you have never done before. This was like a memorial stone to look back on and remind yourself of all I did and all I will do in the future."

We arrived in Cairo in the middle of the night, worn out, but so thankful that God had worked out what seemed like an impossible situation. The next day we did some leadership training with our Egyptian National President and her board, we had wonderful fellowship, and enjoyed the delightful cuisine of our hostesses. We visited the ancient pyramids, rode camels and prayed for this nation. The Christians in that nation do not have it easy. They suffer much persecution, but their zeal and commitment was very inspiring to us. We did not want to leave our sisters, but we had many other places to visit.

The traffic in Cairo was unbelievable! I definitely would not want to drive in that city, but I suppose you get use to it. The national president and her husband drove us to the airport but were not allowed to go in with us. It was emotional saying our good-byes as God had knit our hearts together in a way that only He can do. We were getting our luggage checked when my traveling friend realized she had left her bag with her teaching notes in the trunk of our friends' car. This seemed like déjà vu!

We called the home of our host and talked to her mother who was not a young woman. She explained that her daughter was going to her brother's house, he did not have a phone, and he lived on the other side of town. With that we knew we would have to leave those things behind. But God had a plan.

About the time we were getting on the shuttle to board our plane, a man stepped on the shuttle, called out my name, and said our luggage had arrived. My friend was a runner so she quickly jumped off the shuttle and ran back into the main lobby of the terminal. The shuttle drove off and dropped me and the other passengers at the plane. Now I was all alone. Rather than find my seat, I stood at the door with one foot inside the plane and one foot outside on the steps. I was determined I would not sit down until I knew my traveling partner was going with me. In a few minutes she was dropped off by the shuttle. We got seated, fastened our seat belts, and once again thanked God for watching over us. Now we were on our way to South Africa. I felt like I wanted to pinch myself to see if this was really happening!

It was a year or so later when we found out what happened, how her bag was returned to her. The elderly mother, of our host, had gotten in her car, drove through that horrendous traffic, and told her daughter what had happened. They quickly left the home of her brother and drove back to the airport just in time to get that bag to us before we departed. Another divine intervention of God. We were certainly keeping the angels busy!

Our first stop in South Africa was in Johannesburg. We stayed in the home of our South African national president. She was housing us in an upper bedroom and, remember, I had that enormous suitcase. I wasn't sure I could carry that thing up those stairs. Not only did I have all my clothes, but had brought so many useless things along as well. Grace was looking at me and I knew right away that she had sized me up already and knew I would never get that humongous piece of luggage up the stairs. Without a word she lifted that thing up, threw it on her back, and off she sprinted! I was impressed! I knew Grace was a strong leader but had no idea how physically strong she was. She later laughed and said she would always remember me and my suitcase. I had made an unforgettable, or was it an unforgivable impression! Believe me, after that I started unloading everything that was not absolutely necessary and shipped it back to the Aglow office.

At the time I was in South Africa, apartheid was a big problem. Many of the homes had high walls built around them to protect the residents. Grace was in the process of building a six foot stone wall around her home and doing it alone! But even with the difficult problem of racial segregation, God was using Aglow to break down many walls and barriers among the women.

We traveled with the entire South African national

World, Here We Come

board up the eastern coast and met with leaders at several different places. On our way, we stopped several times, sat on the huge boulders drank hot coffee or tea the women had brought, snacked on cookies, and enjoyed the beauty of the Indian Ocean. We did some sightseeing and saw many beautiful places along our way; we made friends with lovely women from across the oceans.

From there we traveled into western Africa and visited several different nations. We went to Blantyre, Malawi where Aglow was holding their third national conference. The first few days we stayed in the home of the national president of Malawi. Her husband was a scientist studying the diseases of macadamia nuts and that was why they were in Malawi. They were a lovely family and Nora was doing a great job with Aglow. They were excited about holding this conference.

Often the protocol in different nations requires inviting the dignitaries in that particular nation to come and open their meetings. Mama Iamamda was like the first lady of Malawi. The president of Malawi was not married, but Mama Iamamda served in that capacity so she was invited to come and give the opening address at the conference. I was a little nervous about meeting someone of her importance. It was fairly cool that evening and we had to go outside to wait for her driver to bring her to the meeting. I had to learn the proper way to greet this dignitary.

We stood in the cool air for quite awhile before her chauffer-driven Mercedes drove up and dropped her off. My hands were freezing by the time she got there. I shook her hand, greeted her with a small curtsy and she grabbed my hand, held it for a moment, and said, "Oh my dear, I am so sorry I made you wait in the cold for me." I immediately felt a connection with this lovely woman. She seemed so down to earth.

Mama Iamamda opened the meeting and then I spoke. I was nervous but I gave a brief message on how God was using women to change the world. I had several interesting stories to tell and felt it was a good word. After I sat down she whispered in my ear, "Could I have a copy of your notes?" I was flattered and encouraged. After the meeting we were making small talk and she said, "I want to have a tea in your honor at the palace." I gulped and said something, not even sure what, but I could not believe that I was going to be entertained in a palace.

Now I have to tell you something interesting. Years ago, (years and years ago in fact) it was my 16th birthday and my parents always indulged me with generous gifts even though we were not a wealthy family. What do you suppose my mother gave me on this important birthday? A book of etiquette. Being the spoiled brat that I was, I let my mother know in uncertain terms that I was not pleased with that gift! Being raised in the South, it was quite important for me to learn good manners. My mother was not educated, but she wanted to do everything she could to help me mature into a proper young lady. She introduced me to good books, music, the arts, and then she wanted to make sure that I knew what to do no matter where I might be. In other words, if I happened to be at a formal gathering, perhaps having dinner, she wanted to make sure I knew which fork to use and when. And with that in mind she presented me with that ugly old book of etiquette and when I opened this and questioned why she would give me something like that she said, "Elaine, you never know what you might be doing in life. You might even be in a palace some day." I wish my mother could have lived long enough to hear my story of being entertained in this gorgeous palace. She would have loved it and then she would have said something like this, "Elaine, mothers always know best."

We were escorted to the palace in a chauffer driven limousine and I felt so elegant! It was like a fairy tale for me. Mama Iamanda greeted me with her beautiful smile and a warm embrace. She had invited several women from the conference to attend. First of all we went outside and the grounds were absolutely gorgeous! The palace sat on a hill that overlooked the city. Everything was green and lush. There were many African women dressed in their native dress and they gathered in a circle and began to dance around us. It was breathtaking. Mama Iamanda insisted I dance with them so I reluctantly did. Others also started dancing and we had a wonderful time. It was such fun!

Then we went back inside the palace and were served a lovely light lunch. The food was not only beautiful to see, but also quite tasty. They had a large, elaborately decorated cake and she asked me to cut the cake, then servants walked around and served each person. I sat there almost in a daze thinking how God had provided all this for his daughters. I remembered a word someone had given me several years before. My friend prophesied that one day I would be entertained in a palace. I have to say I really thought my friend was just talking out of her own desire for me. Little did I know what God had in mind when He put me in this position.

We left Malawi and traveled to several other nations in western Africa. We spent quite a bit of time in Ghana. They, too, were having a national conference and had women coming from other places. We started the services around 9:30, but the women gathered hours before the service would start. Many of the women had their babies with them and carried them on their back or chest in little slings. It was amazing how quiet these babies were. We seldom heard them cry out and yet they were there for hours. The conference would not end until later at night and yet these same women would arrive very early in the morning. They were worshippers!

I had always been a very spontaneous speaker. Often I would arrive at a meeting and not have a clue what I was going to speak on, but I was always confident that God would give me a word for that particular group and He always did. But now, traveling outside the United States, things were different. In many of the nations I would need an interpreter. Some would request a copy of my notes so they could get familiar with my message. Notes? I never used them, but I knew it was necessary, so I started writing out my messages. During the conference in Ghana, I had two interpreters at the same time. One spoke in French for the French-speaking women and the other spoke in a native dialect that was familiar for several of the other attendees. I would have to pause for a few seconds to give each interpreter time to interpret. Frankly I was thankful I had notes because it was easy

World, Here We Come

to forget what I had just said by time both interpreters finished.

The conference was wonderful and I loved the enthusiasm of the women! Here in the United States we begin to get uncomfortable if a service lasts over two hours. The African women would have stayed all night if the meetings would last that long. They were hungry and never seemed to get enough! God really gave me a heart for the African women. I loved them! Several years later when I was retiring from Aglow, we were meeting with our national leaders and the national president of Ghana at that time came up and draped a beautiful tribal cloth over my shoulders she said, "Elaine, you have been a healing bond between the African woman and the white woman." I was already emotional as this would be my last time with the leaders of the international field and I burst out bawling like a baby! After all those years, I was still amazed that God had allowed me to serve in this position.

We stayed in the home of the national president of Ghana and her husband was running for the presidency of this country. They were a lovely and godly couple. We would often hear them praying and worshipping together in the mornings. Unfortunately he was not elected, but he was already doing many things to improve the conditions of his country. He had a huge chicken farm and employed hundreds of people. He also had a small clinic and provided medical care for his employees. After being in Ghana for several days, it was time to leave and move to another nation. Once again we were leaving a part of our heart in that beautiful country.

We continued to travel to several more nations and

Living Expectantly

were able to meet with our wonderful leaders. Each group seemed excited to have us visit their country and of course we were also excited. We trained leaders, did some problem solving, prayed for the people and their Aglow groups, after several weeks it was time to go back home. As much as we enjoyed our trip we were excited to board the plane and head for the United States! As the saying goes, "there is no place like home." I know our husbands were ready to have us back home and we were happy to see them, but we had made memories that would linger in our hearts forever!

A few years after we moved to Seattle, Bill decided to enroll in a Bible college. This was something he had always desired as he wanted to finish his education that had been interrupted when we got married. Though he was older he loved learning and made excellent grades. He graduated with a degree in Christian Education and later got his masters in Christian Counseling.

He also did some traveling overseas and like myself, loved going to other nations. His first outreach trip was to Poland. From 1945 to 1989, Poland, like many other nations, had been under the dominance of the Soviet Union. They experienced increasing economic and political difficulties, and the people were not allowed to worship freely in their own churches. If you recall, in 1987 President Ronald Reagan was meeting with Mikhail Gorbachev and boldly stated, "Mr. President, tear down that wall!"

What a surprise to awake on the morning of November 9, 1989, and hear the news that the Berlin Wall had come down! This was a history-making event and ended

World, Here We Come

what was known as the Cold War. No longer would eastern and western Europe be separated. The wall was down! We Aglow women were ecstatic at this news as we had been praying for years for this to happen. In fact, several Aglow women traveled to Eastern Europe right before this happened and their sole purpose was to pray for the wall to come down! Prayers had been answered!

When Bill and this team traveled to Poland, it was only a few years after the wall had come down and the nation was still struggling to recover. They were quite poor and unable to get many things that were necessary for survival. This team carried in medical supplies, clothes, Bibles, and other things to bless the people. Pastors were now free to proclaim the Gospel, but they did not have proper clothes. Several of the men on the team left suits, shoes, and ties behind when they departed from Poland. They were able to lead several people to the Lord and it was a wonderful experience for Bill. Several years later he made his second trip to Poland. He loved the people and wanted to connect with them once again.

My intercessor and I also traveled to Poland while we were doing an outreach trip to several different nations

We walked the streets of Poland and prayed for God to invade the hearts and land of these people.

---

in Europe. We purposely went there in the hope of seeing an Aglow group established there eventually. We walked the streets of Poland and prayed for God to invade the hearts and land of these people. Economically,

Poland was still recovering. It was quite common to see people on the streets selling whatever they could in order to survive. It was an interesting trip for us and our hearts were touched and saddened to think about all these people had gone through and the way they had been deprived in many ways and for many years. Let us never take our freedom for granted!

Leaving My Thumbprint on the Nations

As I traveled, people often asked me which nation was my favorite. That is a hard question to answer as there are many places that I love for different reasons. I do have to say Mongolia will always hold a special place in my heart. Why? One reason is that the people were so needy and so hungry. When you prepare a "meal" there's nothing more discouraging, than to discover no one was hungry. Do you know what I mean? The Mongols were hungry.

I was able to visit that country twice. The first time we were there we discovered there were only one hundred known Christians in that nation. Also, at that time they did not have a Bible in their language, although someone was translating the New Testament which they were able to get a few years later. On our first trip, we took a team in to specifically pray for the nation. Three men from different ministries traveled with Jane and myself, along with three other leaders from Aglow. We all had one thing in common: we wanted to see the Gospel break forth in this third world nation.

Leaving My Thumbprint on the Nations

Although we were staying in the capital city of Ulaanbaatar, we wanted to go out to the countryside to walk the land and pray. Nick and his family, were originally from Canada but had lived in Mongolia for a number of years. He was a great help in taking us to key places to pray. One place in particular was the convent for monks. It was surrounded by fences, but we were able to crawl under the fence and once we got on the property we walked the land. Fortunately this was at a time that the monks were not in residence. We wrote out scriptures and dug holes and planted God's word. One of the gentlemen with us felt the Lord told him one day this land would belong to the Christians and would become a retreat site.

We made declarations and declared, *"Every place on which the sole of your foot treads, I have given it to you."* (JOSHUA 1:3) A few years later, Jane and I returned to Mongolia and were able to start an Aglow group. On this trip, we ministered to men, women, and children. We met in a building that had formerly been used by the Soviets for their meetings. And now God was using this place for His glory. God was raining on this dry, parched desert land.

Another place that stands out as being special place is Russia. Again, people were so hungry. I believe it was 1990 when a team of us went to Russia. That was shortly after the Berlin Wall had come down. After being in captivity for so long, you can imagine how eager the women were to hear the word of God and have the opportunity to worship freely. We went to several places while in Russia, but I'll always remember my time in Siberia.

There were five of us traveling together and we stayed in peoples' homes. This is always exciting as you get a first-hand look at how the people actually live. I stayed with Larissa, a lovely Russian lady who taught English at the university.

Once the people had the freedom to worship, ministries were coming from everywhere to preach the Gospel; the harvest was ripe for picking. Because Larissa taught English, and spoke perfect English, she was being

> **Once the people had the freedom to worship, ministries were coming from everywhere to preach the Gospel.**

used by many ministries to interpret. As she was interpreting, she started hearing the word of God and Holy Spirit was opening her heart to Truth. She thought that one of her students at the university was a Christian, so she asked him if he had a Bible she could borrow. He did and she took it home and started devouring the word of God.

It wasn't long until she began to understand what it meant to be born again and to be water baptized. Larissa gave her heart to Jesus and even baptized herself in her bathtub. She was very hungry to learn more about God and we had some wonderful conversations while I was able to be in her home. I'll never forget the meal she had prepared for me when I first got to her home. She sat and talked to me while I ate. I kept inviting her to join me but she would politely say she wasn't hungry. Later I found out she didn't eat because she wanted to make sure I, her guest, had plenty to eat.

The room that I slept in was so dimly lit that I could barely see to read. I wondered why she didn't put a stronger bulb in the lamp, but then I found out light bulbs were either scarce or unavailable. Her brother-in-law was in the military and later while I was still there, Larissa's sister brought her some new light bulbs. Here in America we have no idea what others do without as we are blessed with so much abundance.

A couple of the women I was traveling with were from England and they had carried in fur coats to give to the Russian women. In England, women rarely wear any type of fur as animal activists throw paint on their furs to protest the wearing of animal fur. These were not new fur coats, but they were still in excellent condition and provided such warmth for the women in their extreme winters. We were there in January and we had to walk to some of the meeting places. One evening as we walked back to our homes from the meeting, the temperature was 19 degrees below zero. Fortunately, I managed to stay warm as I had heavy fur lined boots and a fur hat that had been loaned to me.

During our time in Siberia, we met an Aglow leader that had a ministry of helping women that were being released from prison. Two of these women were in her home at that time. In Siberia, once you had been in prison you were unable to seek employment. These particular women had been arrested for stealing food and a pair of shoes. Ludell, the Aglow leader, had acquired an old factory building and somehow was able to purchase industrial type sewing machines. She opened a sewing factory in order for released prisoners to have jobs. Now, they needed fabric, and Aglow International had sent out a request for the women of the field to gather material so it could be sent to Siberia.

You can imagine the excitement and enthusiasm of the women as they went to work gathering fabric from their areas. The amount they were able to collect was phenomenal. Now the problem was how to get it to the women across the sea. God is good and He had gone before them and already had provision in place. Someone had connections with a gentlemen in Europe that purchased cars from the United States and he agreed to help them. Not only was he willing to ship this cargo at his own expense, but offered them an enormous storage vat to store the material in and he would ensure it was delivered to the designated place.

In the meantime, someone contacted Aglow with an offer of a well-know brand of baby food that was available for free. There were many cases of this food. The expiration date was past, but according to the company, the food was good for another year or two. What a convenient time to hear about this offer. Have you already guessed what they did? They put the cases of baby food in the vat, padded it with the fabric, and this was shipped to the sewing factory in Siberia.

This shipment of baby food and fabric was delivered shortly before I arrived. When we visited the sewing factory, we were able to see what God had done. Not only had He provided fabric so these ex-prisoners would be able to have an income from their sewing projects, but He had also provided tons of food for the babies of this community. What a witness this was to these mothers that did not have the money to purchase the food their children needed. Yes! We serve an amazing God and so creative in all He does!

At the first Aglow International Conference after the wall had come down, we were able to bring five women from Moscow to attend the conference. The Aglow women had made Russia a priority in prayer for years and when these five women walked down the aisle carrying the flag from their nation, the attendees went wild! It was a Hallelujah Wingding . . . that's another one of those Texas sayings, but believe it or not you will find this word in your dictionary! The women were dancing, crying, and praising God for what He had done! It was a moment that I never want to forget.

I will say this for Aglow women, they are warriors when it comes to prayer. They seem to know how to reach the heart of God. Several years ago, God began to put it on the heart of our leaders to pray for the Muslim women. At one of our conferences, our speaker, Rick Joyner, who is well-known in the Body of Christ, interrupted his message, turned to Jane, our president, and said, "Jane, God will give you Islam if you will take it!" He had no idea what he was speaking to her, he was only being obedient to God, but God was using him to confirm to Aglow what their next mandate would be. Since that time, Aglow has made massive inroads into the dark kingdom of the Islamic world. *"I permitted Myself to be found by those who did not seek Me, I said, 'Here am I, here am I,"* ISAIAH 65:1.

My intercessor, who had become a good friend,

brought teams of women to the Aglow office to pray for our staff. It was a mutual blessing for all involved. The women loved coming to the office and our staff loved having the women come and pray for them. One particular time, she invited a well-known woman who moved mightily in the Holy Spirit to come out and speak and minister to the staff. This woman had quite a reputation for hearing accurately from God, and Bill and I had the privilege of hosting her in our home.

She knew nothing about my position in Aglow, she only knew I worked at the office. She gave me a beautiful word and one thing she said that touched me was, "You will leave your thumbprint on the nations." She had no idea that in my position I traveled to the nations. Then she gave Bill a wonderful, encouraging word. She told him how the devil had tried to wipe him out through death and yet, how God was using him to touch the lives of men. But then she said something that I wasn't sure was from God. Later after she had left our home, I told Bill, "She was right on, but that thing she said about Kyle . . . I'm just not sure about."

At that time, Kyle was far away from God and having prayed long and hard without seeing any results it seemed like it would never happen. But she said, "you have a young son that you are concerned about, but in a moment God will make him a man of stability." Remember how Sarah laughed to herself when the Lord told Abraham his wife would bear a son from her own body? (GENESIS 18:10–12) That was how I was feeling when Bill got that word. Like Sarah, it looked so impossible in the natural, but it wasn't long until Kyle returned to the Lord and God made him a man of stability, one that knew what he wanted to do with his life. It was one of those "suddenly" things that only God can do.

After serving fourteen years with Aglow in Seattle, Bill and I were beginning to sense it was time to return to Ohio. We had been praying about it and as much as I loved this job and the people, I was felt this was God prompting us to start making plans. We would need to sell our house before we could move back and we had talked about putting a "for sale by owner" sign out front before we even listed the house to see what would happen.

One day Bill came in and said, "I'm going to run an ad in the little neighborhood paper and see if we get any calls." I immediately started telling him that was not a good idea, that no one purchases houses from ads in neighborhood papers. Well, it was a good thing my husband did exactly what he thought he should do because once the ad came out we immediately got a phone call. This person knew the area and was wanting a house in our locale. She came out the next day, loved the place, brought her brother back the next day to look the house over, and offered us exactly what we were asking. And would you believe this? We never even put the "for sale" sign up. What is that scripture that says, *"Wives adapt yourself to your husband, learn to adapt."* (EPHESIANS 5:22) (JBP) Hmm, I guess that really works, right?!?

We had sold our house, but I had not even talked to Jane, my boss, about the possibility of our moving, and we had no house in Ohio yet. Fortunately, the buyer was in no hurry to move so that relieved our minds, but we had already made plans to go back to Ohio for a little vacation and while there we bought a house. Ohio, ready or not, here we come. Things were moving quickly—quicker than I felt we were ready. It was the year for our international conference and my department had a lot of responsibility to get ready for that event. After moving, I went back out to the office in Seattle several times for two weeks at a time in order to do all that was needed.

We had a big garage sale, packed boxes for weeks, and finally headed back to Ohio. Remember how I wrote about our move to Seattle and how I cried and cried? Well, this was no different except this time we were going back to where we had come from. Believe me, my heart felt divided. I loved the women in Seattle that had now become so precious to me, but at the same time I loved my children and was eager to get back with them. And I wanted to be with my grandchildren. It was a bittersweet time.

I happened upon a scripture that reminded me of where I was at that moment—please allow me grace to change a few things that make it apropos for my situation. This is found in Genesis 32:10 and it's the story of Jacob as he was returning to Bethel. God had promised Jacob when he left Bethel that one day he would return (GEN. 28:15) We always knew we would return to Ohio, that our time in Seattle was only for a season. And now we knew it was time to return to our former home. *"I am unworthy of all the loving kindness and of all the faithfulness which you have shown Your servant, for with my staff only I crossed this Jordan, and now I have become two companies."* Now I realize that Jacob was about to meet up with his brother Esau and he was very afraid of that meeting, but that part had nothing to do with me. How this verse spoke to me was this way: I feel Jacob was pouring his heart out to the Lord and was grateful for all the kindness God had poured out to him. He felt he went out there with nothing, but came back with so much more. That was what I was feeling. Jacob said all he had was a staff when he went out there; not very much obviously. But now as he was returning he saw all God had added to him. Those were my sentiments exactly.

When I went to Aglow, I felt I had so little to offer and yet, for whatever reason, God had opened this door of opportunity. Now that I was leaving, I felt so much had been added to my life. Jacob said he had returned with two companies; in other words, he was returning with so much more than what he left with. That was me. The people I met, the things I learned, the experiences I had, the forty plus nations I was able to visit and the awesome opportunity I had to leave my thumbprint on each of them. It was more than I could have ever asked or hoped for. Surely, God is the God of much more!

We moved back to Ohio in July. One of the things we were concerned about when we decided to come back was our health insurance. I knew I could continue with my present insurance for six months, but after that time I would have to find another carrier. At our age it could pose a problem to get good insurance without having to pay an exorbitant price. Now it was January and time to find another insurance company and we were a little nervous. You know how ole' slew foot will start trying to make you doubt God, doubt whether or not you did the right thing in making that move, right? Or, are we the only ones he works on like that?

I was beginning to feel a little apprehensive about all of this, but God in His goodness and mercy sent me a wonderful note on that particular day. In the mail I received a letter from the Prayer Coordinator of Nicaragua. I wasn't even sure I had ever met her, but she had written me a note. The interesting thing was, this note had been written shortly after my announcement of leaving Aglow, about June or July. Because it was written in Spanish, our translator at Aglow had to translate it. Since I was no longer with Aglow, getting it translated was not a priority, so I did not receive it until January of the next year. The woman began to tell me how sorry she was to hear of my leaving, etc. Apparently she had ended the letter and left for her office. After a while she began to feel in the spirit that she needed to write more. I wish I had the letter before me. For whatever reason I'm unable to find the letter, but I will relate this as best as I recall having read it over and over so many times.

She went on to say that as much as she hated to see me leave, she felt an urgent need to send me this scripture. And here was the scripture, Luke 8:39. Once again, please allow me to change the he to she so that it will be more personal and that was the way this woman wrote it out in her note. If you would read the bottom portion of the scripture, verse 38, you will see it was Jesus speaking and He said, *"Return to your house and describe what great things God has done for you." So she went away and proclaiming throughout the whole city what great things*

Jesus had done for her.

That was all I needed. With Jesus telling me Himself to return to my house, why should I worry or fret about such a small thing as insurance? Every detail of my life was being taken care of by Him. He had sent us back and as He always had, He would provide!

That's what I mean when I encourage you to **Live Expectantly**. You don't have to wait until you reach heaven to see the goodness of the Lord. He wants to reveal **Himself** to you right now, right where you are.

Coming Out of Hiding

It was great being back home with our family, but there were many things I missed about Aglow. I still marvel how God supernaturally opened that door for me. I experienced many unexpected opportunities that were life changing for me. But now I missed my friends that I made and being on the cutting edge of all God was doing.

At the time that I worked at the international office, there were eight of us that served as corporate officers. Jane, our president, was the head CEO and the rest of us were vice presidents heading up individual departments. We worked closely together and as a result, for the most part, we become close. Several times we would take time away from the office and have relationship building weekends. Because we were on the front line of ministry, it was important for us to keep our hearts right and deal with issues that could become a stumbling block and even affect the ministry.

I remember one of the first times we got away for a little retreat. Jane's office had planned some activities that were designed to help break down any walls or barriers that we might have built. This could become a very intimate time as we were learning to be open and honest with one another. I had never experienced anything like this and, as I had said earlier, "I was a talker, but I never talked out of my heart." I didn't have a clue what my true feelings were. Growing up, I had learned to stuff my feelings. If I did try to express what I felt, no one listened to me or they would tell me I shouldn't feel that way. It was during these times of openness with our board, that God began to bring down many walls I had erected. This was not easy for me and occasionally those dormant feelings would come to the surface and I did not have a clue what to do with them.

At one of our little gatherings, colored squares of paper were laid out and we were instructed to pick up different colors, whatever appealed to us. Later we went around the room and shared the emotion we felt the color best represented. When it came my turn to share I had chosen a red square and a black square, I said I felt the black was depression and fear, the red was anger. I didn't realize at the time I chose the squares that they were the emotions I was struggling with. As I began to talk, I also started crying. I was slowly getting in touch with some deeply hidden emotions that I had never expressed openly. For the most part, I laughed a lot, cut up, and had what appeared to be a very jovial attitude, but what I was discovering—underneath the "fig leaves" is that there was much anger and other hidden emotions.

Once I became a Christian, I seldom shared when I felt depression, and I was depressed more than I like to admit. Even as a teen I often struggled with depression but had learned to hide it behind my laughter. I did open up at different times and would admit to my depressed state, only to be told, "Christians should not have depression." With those kind of remarks, I learned to push these things down and cover with my fig leaves. I personally feel we all need someone or someplace where we can be real, gut-level honest, if you will. It is a real treasure when you find someone with whom you can be totally honest and know that you are still loved and respected. We each need a safe place where we can remove the fig leaves and know someone will cover our nakedness and

> **When I speak of being honest, this does not mean we tell everyone everything, but it is finding that person with whom you feel comfortable and know they are trustworthy.**

not expose us. When I speak of being honest, this does not mean we tell everyone everything, but it is finding that person with whom you feel comfortable and know they are trustworthy. I will always be grateful for those years I was at the Aglow International Office, serving with such Godly and honorable women; women like myself that were wanting to be whole in every area of their life. Yes, we were all leaders and in high places of leadership, but still in need of healing. I received much inner healing during that time, but there were still areas where God wanted to set me free.

Do you remember the Scripture in John 11, the story of Lazarus being raised from the grave? When Jesus was told his friend Lazarus was sick, Jesus purposely delayed coming to him. When He finally did arrive, Lazarus had already died and been buried. Jesus instructed the people to remove the stone that was covering the grave site. Martha, the sister of the dead man, was concerned. Lazarus had been in the grave four days and there was a strong smell emanating from the grave. This did not deter the plan Jesus had. Jesus said with a loud voice, "Lazarus, come forth!" And Lazarus, still in his grave clothes, came forth from the grave. Then Jesus turned to the people and said, "You unwrap him!"

I believe Jesus was demonstrating something that we need to know. Before we come to know Jesus, we are in a "grave" of sorts. We may be alive, but we are not full of the life He intended for us. Once the stone is rolled away and Jesus calls us forth, His intent is to use us to unwrap others. Jesus could have unwrapped Lazarus, but for whatever reason, we are to unwrap one another. Yes, it can be dirty, stinky, unpleasant, time consuming, but helpful, and of course, healing! Jesus is so patient, He doesn't allow us to be unwrapped all at once, but as we are ready and willing He sends someone to take off another grave cloth. In our position, our place in Christ, we are perfect. In our performance, we are becoming. It is a process.

It was my desire from the first day I surrendered to Jesus to be whole in every area of my life. I knew I needed healing and I have been open to whatever and whenever He prompts me to get help. I feel I have come a long way, but I also am aware I'm not where I need to be. Philippians 1:6 tells us, *"For I am confident of this very thing, that He who began a good work in you will perfect it until the day of Christ Jesus."* I don't believe it is up to us to start searching, as God will begin to show us when we need to look at something. He is capable of bringing things to the surface when needed. As we see in Jeremiah 17:10 He says, *"I, the Lord, search the heart."*

Something had been stirring in my own heart, not only while I was in Seattle, but more so since moving back around our family. This was something that had been hidden for years. It seemed to be surfacing and I began to question if it was time to bring this forth. Should this secret finally be exposed to the light? It wasn't that I hadn't talked about this to a few people over the years, but now I felt I needed to share this with my family. I was fully aware that by bringing it out in the open I would be taking a great risk. What would my children think of their mother whom I felt they trusted as having been very honest with them all these years? These were the things I needed to consider and yet, in my heart of hearts, I felt it was time to come out of hiding.

I wrote a letter to a well-known Christian psychologist, explaining my problem. He put me in touch with a pastor on his staff. The pastor called and I felt very comfortable with him and knew he had much wisdom. Because this continued to nag at my heart, the pastor agreed that it was time for me to share with my children and their spouses. He wanted to make sure Bill was on board with me and he was. I have to confess, I was dreading that moment. I knew many things could be at stake. It was one thing to share with my children, but what would their spouse think? I felt I needed to share with each couple, not just each child. Would everyone totally lose respect for me? But on the other hand, what if I died and then this secret came out, what then? I couldn't bear the thought that my children would think I had deceived them all these years. After all, I had tried so hard to teach them to be open, honest, and truthful, and then to think their own mother had been hiding for so long—living a lie, so to speak! I knew what I had to do and I also knew I had to trust God would work all things out.

As I have mentioned several times throughout this book, we had brought a lot of baggage into our marriage. There were things we had never dealt with. When we don't deal with the things, we are burying them alive and eventually they will rise up to haunt us. I felt that was where I was. My past had caught up with me.

Of course Bill knew about this before we married and we had talked about it many times. He was in total agreement with me whether I told the children or not. It did not matter to him, but he could see that it was beginning to deeply trouble me and perhaps the time had come to share the truth with our family. We both were questioning how they would react. We had hoped to tell all three couples together, but with one couple living out of state, we begin to see we would have to tell each couple individually. Where do you start to unravel such a big lie? We never deliberately set out to deceive anyone, it just happened. Let me try and explain.

Bill and I met while he was attending university in the city where I lived and grew up. I was still in high school when we first saw one another at an event. Though we did not speak to one another, we noticed one another and somehow connected. I jokingly said to my girlfriends that were with me, "That is the guy I'm going

Living Expectantly

to marry!" Several weeks passed and one afternoon while working at the downtown theatre box office, I "happened" to see this handsome fellow across the street and knew immediately it was the same guy I had seen earlier. About that time he spotted me and our eyes locked. He walked across the street, came up to the box office, we exchanged pleasantries, talked a few minutes, and that was that. I don't believe we even exchanged names.

Another few weeks passed and I was walking down the street in the downtown area when someone whistled at me. I had been taught that nice girls never turned around when a fellow whistled, so I kept walking, but this person caught up with me and guess who it was? The same fellow I had run into twice before and now I found out his name was Bill. Was that fate, or was it a divine meeting arranged by God? Who's to say? Bill's parents had come to town and they were shopping. Bill insisted I come into the men's clothing store and meet his parents. I met them and was impressed. They were quite nice and a very handsome couple. I could see where Bill got his good looks. At that point we exchanged phone numbers, or I should say he got my phone number. In my young days, a girl would never have thought of calling a guy—that is, a nice girl! Yep! For you younger readers, that was in the dark ages, about 100 years ago. But, seriously, most girls—and especially my friends—would have never called a guy. This was the beginning of an on again, off again relationship, probably more off than on!

Obviously we were quite attracted to one another. Eventually we thought we were in love. Bill's father suggested we were only infatuated with one another.

According to Webster's, that would mean: completely carried away by foolish or shallow love or affection. Thinking back, that probably does more aptly describe where we were at the time. Bill was an only child and I was like an only child as my only sibling, a brother, was nine years older than me. We were both quite self-centered, spoiled, and very emotionally immature. But the sparks flew between us, the fires of lust, and the fires of war!

Many years later we learned about arrested development. When a person has been emotionally injured, they normally only grow two years past the time the "injury" happened. Understanding this now, neither of us at that time were more than 11–12 years old in our emotional development! Certainly not ready for any serious relationship, but we were "in love."

We became intimate. In other words, we were having sex outside of marriage. Today this seems to be the norm for many young people. Certainly it is not right in the eyes of God, but it is accepted in today's society and even in some Christian homes. But in the time I grew up, it was almost the unpardonable sin! I knew better, my mother had done all she knew to do to teach me right from wrong, to make right choices, but being quite stubborn and rebellious at that time, I was doing my own thing! As I have ministered to women through the years, I have never had one woman to tell me she regretted saving herself for her husband, but I have had hundreds that wished they had waited till they married. God wasn't trying to be mean and keep us from something beautiful that He had planned, but it is sort of like opening a Christmas present before the intended time. Yes, you would still enjoy it, but the awesomeness of it is lost.

Often Bill and I would talk about getting married, but I was still in high school and not sure I was ready to settle down, besides we fought a lot. We were both quite jealous of one another and I had caught Bill in several lies concerning his dating other girls, but in spite of all this we continued to date. By now summer had rolled around and Bill was returning to his home town where he had a summer job. He would return to school for his junior year in the fall. I had graduated and enrolled in college—not the same one as Bill, but fairly close. I had gotten a job at a bank and planned to work there until I started school. Before Bill had gone back home we had a big fight and were no longer seeing one another. I really found myself missing him, but was too stubborn to let him know.

During this time, I met another fellow and started seeing him. It was not a good relationship and I knew it, but for whatever reason I was attracted to this fellow. He was a few years older, out of college, and wise in the ways of the world. He was sophisticated, urbane, and had been around. Believe it or not, I was fairly innocent in many ways. In one sense, I had led a very protected life as far as being exposed to a lot of worldliness. Not only this, but he had a serious drinking problem, and though I never cared for hard liquor, I began drinking along with him. Eventually we became intimate and I became pregnant. Even as I am writing the account of my story, I can still feel the emotions that rose up in me when I discovered this. What was I to do? How could I explain this to my parents? How could I bring such shame on my family? This guy had expressed his love for me and of course I believed him, but when I told him I was pregnant everything changed. He immediately suggested I get something from the pharmacy that would take care of this "problem."

I will say, I never got the product. I'm not sure what it was or what it would do, but I assumed it would probably cause me to abort. At that time, abortions were illegal. Of course there were places where you could go, but it would have been risky and dangerous. As I have thought of this since then, I questioned whether I would have gotten an abortion had it been accessible to me. I don't think so. Though I was not walking with the Lord at this time, I always felt abortion was wrong and knew this was not just a fetus or a blob of tissue as so many are taught today, it was a baby. But, I also knew something else. This fellow that had professed to love me, had only used me for his fleshly pleasures and now I was ALONE and absolutely petrified! I did not know what to do or where to turn.

I was working and because I was very thin I was able to hide the pregnancy. At this point I had not told my parents, but I knew at some time I would have to tell them and I knew it would not be an easy thing to do. As much as I loved my mother and she loved me, I was afraid she would not be supportive and I knew she would be furious! I did not want to face her wrath. In the meantime, Bill started calling me again and we began seeing each other. And as we had talked in the past, he brought up the subject of our getting married. Now I had to tell him my deep, dark secret! Naturally he was mad. Mad because I had been seeing someone—although he too had been dating—and really mad because of the way this guy had treated me. I had not heard another word from this guy since I had told him I was pregnant and he was the father.

Bill continued to insist that we marry and raise this child as our own. Finally, we decided to do this and no one needed to know otherwise. We announced to both sets of parents our plans. We were going to get married and we wanted to get married right away. Both parents were thrilled. My parents loved Bill and I believe his parents loved me as well, but I knew they had been mad at me when we broke up because I had hurt their son. Anyway, we had their blessing and we began to plan a wedding.

It wasn't long until I began to show and Bill's father suspected something since we had been broken up for several months prior to this time. My mother and I were at Bill's home with his parents when the truth came out. It was awful, so humiliating, and my poor mother was so embarrassed and angry. Up to this time she had either gone into denial that I could be pregnant or had never noticed. At one time she had questioned me, but of course I lied. Did she believe me or did she move into total denial? I'll never know. Bill and I confessed our plan to marry and that Bill had agreed to father another man's child. His parents tried their best to convince him he should not do this, or at least wait, but Bill was adamant. He loved me, we loved each other, and wanted to marry right away!

Coming Out of Hiding

So our parents, or I should say Bill's parents and my mother, came up with a plan. We could go ahead and marry, but I had to surrender the baby for adoption. As I mentioned earlier, we were both so terribly immature that we still allowed our parents to order our lives and we agreed to this plan. My mother took me in to see her doctor who confirmed the pregnancy. He and another doctor found a family that was eager to adopt. We made plans to move to another city after our big, formal wedding and pretend that Bill had taken a job for the winter. We were able to concoct a lie that seemed totally feasible and to our knowledge no one ever knew any differently. I walked down the aisle wearing a beautiful white formal wedding gown, had six attendants, and was married in my home church where I seldom attended. We went on a brief honeymoon, came back to our little house that Bill had recently purchased, and started living a lie!

Shortly after this, we closed up our little house in the suburbs and moved to another city. There I lived in total seclusion, never leaving the house lest someone I knew would see me. Bill did have a job, but I never stepped outside our doors. I even had my groceries delivered. Our parents made us promise that I would not leave the house until I gave birth. We were all so afraid someone would see me and discover our secret.

The doctor that was caring for me arranged to come to our apartment for my prenatal care. On the day I went into labor, the doctor and his nurse drove over to our apartment, picked me up, and took me to the hospital. The doctor did not know I was married, so Bill could not come to the hospital with me. My parents came down in time for me to give birth. My mother did not call me by my name while I was in the hospital but an assumed name. So many lies were told in order to cover the shame I had brought on my family! I was afraid, but still it was nothing we talked about. It was as if I was there to deliver a "product" to someone and once it was over I could go back home and live a normal life. Whatever normal was going to be after this. At that time most women did not give birth naturally, we were sedated. I gave birth to a child I never saw, never held, and was never allowed to know whether it was a boy or girl. I was only the deliverer of the "product" and never mind what was in the "box."

No questions asked . . . just sign on the dotted line and it would all be over and behind me. Both of my parents are now dead, and until their deaths it was something my mother and I never discussed. It was a closed book. My father never asked who the guy was that fathered the child. This was how my family dealt with uncomfortable things. We just swept things under the carpet and hoped the lumps would not become so noticeable we could no longer keep them covered. I have to admit, at that time I really did not have a lot of feelings about the entire thing. I believe I had totally shut down emotionally. I was just thankful we had pulled this off and no one found out. Even my own brother never knew this, never suspected anything. At the time of my mother's death, thirty-five years after I had given birth to this child, I was able to tell my brother this family secret.

Years later, after I had given my heart to the Lord, I began to think about many things and this was one

Coming Out of Hiding

of those things. Occasionally, I would open up and tell a very close friend, but I never told very many. It was as if I needed to get this out in the open. Maybe I was only wanting someone to tell me I was okay and had not committed the unpardonable sin as I thought. I recall the doctor that delivered the baby saying to me as I got ready to leave the hospital, "Elaine, you are not a bad person. You made a mistake." That was comforting to me, as I felt so shameful. I felt I must have been a terrible person to have allowed this to happen and then to be sent away into hiding and never be allowed to discuss it, all these things enforced the lie that I was bad! In fact, I was worse than bad, I was terrible, I was a despicable, shameful person! And this became my identity!

My father died before my mother. We were never very close and I never expected him to open up and talk to me about that time, but I yearned for my mother and I to have a heart to heart talk. Not only did I need her affirmation, but I felt if we could talk, that healing would come to both of us. My mother absolutely adored babies and thinking about it now, I'm sure that it was very hard for her to give up her grandchild. But we never discussed this. Several times I tried to bring up the subject, but she would get too upset and leave the room. She went to her grave with that in her heart. I often wondered if she ever shared it with anyone. I really doubt it. In her eyes, I had done the worst possible thing a young lady could do. I had shamed myself and my family.

You know, shame is an awful thing. It locks you up. It's like a scar on the soul. It's not about what we do or have done, or who we are. In other words; who we think we are as shame becomes our identity. Shame causes us to hate ourselves; we are worthless. Shame says, "I am not good enough, I am less than." Shame always causes us to feel worthless and inadequate. It eats away at our foundation. Shame is not about being fearfully and wonderfully made, it is about being a mistake! Guilt says, "I made a mistake." Shame says, "I am a mistake."

There was so much dysfunction in my life before this happened, but after this, shame became a huge part of my life and I lived with much self-condemnation and self-hatred. Of course, I became skilled at covering myself. I could laugh and cut up and pretend that everything was all right, but inside I was angry and hurting, and wanting and needing help. The beginning of my restoration started when I made Christ the Lord of my

> **The beginning of my restoration started when I made Christ the Lord of my life.**

life. And now I felt that, in order to be whole, I could no longer live under this lie and I needed to "come clean" before my children. They had a half brother or sister somewhere that they knew nothing about and I knew I could no longer deny them having this information.

At the time I relinquished my child for adoption, no one could open those papers, they were sealed and it was a closed subject. Many children born and adopted during that time never knew they were adopted and many parents chose to keep that a secret. I made a vow to myself that I would never look for that person in case they did not know they were adopted. To me, it would be cruel for them to discover that someone other than their "mother" had given birth to them. It was not my place to tell them, but I had always been open to their looking for me. At this writing that has never happened, but I felt it was the right thing to give my children the opportunity to look for their half sibling if they wanted to do so.

Finally, it worked out that we could tell our children all of this. As it turned out, each couple was totally supportive; shocked, but loving and understanding. I did not feel they thought any less of me and that meant so much to me. I gave them permission to search for this unknown sibling if they so desired.

Maybe you're questioning why I am exposing this here. Ever since I became a follower of Jesus, my desire has been to help others, especially women. Through the years, I have come across many women that carry much pain and hurt inside, and I have discovered that as I make myself vulnerable to them, it has helped to free them to talk about where they are. There is an old Jewish proverb that says, "What leaves the heart reaches the heart." Now, you will not find this in the Bible, but think about it. It is so true. When I am able to do this, I see how we can connect and we seem to be on common ground. When the doctor said to me, "Elaine, you are not a bad person, you just made a mistake," I remember saying to him, "Maybe one day I can help other women." Little did I know how prophetic those words would become. That has been my ministry from day one: helping other women. I am trusting that, by telling my story, you too will be able to tell your story and gain freedom.

Because shame keeps a person locked up and bound, once we can start talking about our pain, it is like a release takes place. Have you ever had a boil on your body? I have and believe me, they are not nice. They can be terribly painful. For those of you that don't know what a boil is, it is an inflamed swelling on the skin that is filled with a nasty secretion and it is caused by some type of infection. The only way to release the pain is to lance the boil, cut it open. Lancing is not pain free. It can be extremely painful, but here is the good news: it is the opening of the wound that causes the healing to come.

Dr. Les Parrott II, a professor of clinical psychology at Seattle Pacific University, told an interesting story that happened while on call as a medical psychologist in the burn unit of a hospital. Dr. Parrott said, "I had observed how much pain patients would endure all in the hope of healing. I watched these patients painfully exercise tender limbs with the guidance of a caring rehabilitation therapist. They had accepted the fact that healing would only come through pain." Then Dr. Parrott added, "On the other hand, in working with burn patients who refused the physical therapy, their highest priority was to avoid pain, not to heal."

I've heard it said, "Some people will not change until the pain of remaining the same becomes greater than the pain of change." My prayer for you right now is that you will make a conscious decision to be willing to go through the process of change, whatever that might be, in order to rid yourself of emotional things that are causing pain in your life and keeping you bound.

While writing this book, I have had many emotions

surface and I have to admit there is a longing in my heart that I have not felt until recently. Because I made that vow, I feel I have not allowed myself to be honest with my true feelings. My desire has always been to protect the "child," but now this "child" is an adult and whether they know they are adopted or not, I want to meet them and tell them why I gave them up. I need to know if they are male or female. I want to know what their life has been like. I want them to know me and their half siblings. Is this a selfish desire? I hope not. I want them to meet my husband. He was willing to marry me and raise this child as his own. That was very unselfish on his part.

Not long ago I read a book by a well-known author, R.T. Kendall. The book is called "Believing God." In one chapter he addressed the subject of making vows. He said, "Don't make any vows other than the marriage vow and the vow to be a Christian." He said, "If you've already made them, forget them! Just keep God's word." We are bound to the word before making vows. Then he wrote something else really got my attention. He said, "A vow is nature's way of robbing God of His glory. Vows do the very opposite of what people think they do. A vow is concocted not because of the Spirit's leading, but because it makes us feel better. We then take the fact that we feel better as the Spirit's witness that we are on the right track. We project that good feeling upon the backdrop of God's heart and claim it as His will, when it is almost always nothing more but our own unbelief dressed in self-righteous apparel."

Having read this, I feel that is where I was at the time I made the vow to never look for the child I had given birth to. Looking back it seemed like such a noble decision, but today, older and hopefully wiser, I feel it was pride; it made me feel good. I have now started a search for this person I birthed 59 years ago. I have inquired into several websites that search for adoptive children. Unfortunately, up to this point I have been unsuccessful. According to Texas law, all adoption records are still sealed and because I was not allowed to know the sex of this child, this has made it even more difficult and complicated. There is the possibility they might look for me, maybe they already have. Is it too difficult for God? I think not! I have put this in His hands. He knows what is best for all involved.

As I have been encouraging you to **Live Expectantly**, that is what I am doing at this time. He is able to open doors no man can shut, so this is no big deal for Him. Of course so many years have passed, this person could have passed away, but I trust they are still alive and like myself, wanting to connect with me. As you read this story, I would appreciate your prayers. *"Behold, I am the God of all flesh, is there anything too difficult for Me?"* (JEREMIAH 32:27) And who knows; perhaps if we do connect, I will write another book to share that story.

Eating at the King's Table

I'm sure you've already discovered that I'm a storyteller. My mother and brother were wonderful storytellers and could captivate an audience by their stories. I feel I inherited their genes to tell my stories. Jesus was a storyteller Himself. If you've read the Gospels in the New Testament, you realize He used parables to teach spiritual truths. I've had people tell me from time to time after having heard me speak someplace, "I still remember your story of such and such." There's something about a good story that just seems to stay with you.

One of my favorite stories in the Bible is found in the Old Testament and it is the story of Mephibosheth. Perhaps you are saying, "Who in the world is this person and how do you even pronounce his name?" Mephibosheth was the son of Jonathan, and Jonathan was David's closest friend.

Jonathan was also the son of King Saul and at one time Saul and his men chased David and threatened to kill him. Saul was terribly jealous of David and his popularity and knew one day David would eventually take the throne. Time passed and David continued to run and hide from Saul. During this time Jonathan risked

Eating at the King's Table

his own life to come and encourage his friend, David. He made a covenant with David. (I SAMUEL 18) In their covenant he basically said, "My life is laid down for your protection." He totally committed himself to David. Eventually Saul gave up his pursuit of finding David and in time Saul and his three sons—including—Jonathan—were killed. Scripture tells us that David deeply mourned for both Jonathan and Saul whom he loved. It's a beautiful picture of how God would have us treat even an enemy. (II SAMUEL 1:17)

Before Jonathan's death he had fathered a son, Mephibosheth who was five years old at the time of Jonathan's death. Being the grandson of Saul, his life was at stake. At this time in history, families of deposed dynasties would usually be killed by their successors. When the people within Saul's court heard of his death, their hearts were pierced with fear. In terror they sought safety believing David would seek revenge and kill all of them. The nurse in charge of Mephibosheth hastily picked up the young boy and as they ran to hide, the nurse slipped and fell and the child was crippled from the accident. Fearing for their lives, the servants took this young boy to a place called Lodebar. That was the last we would hear of the child for a number of years. (II SAMUEL 4:4)

Jonathan realized that one day David would be king and he had requested protection for himself and his family once David took the throne. Many years later David was king and he began to search for some descendant of his friend Jonathan. He said, "Is there anyone left that I may show kindness for Jonathan's sake?" (II SAMUEL 9) In those days you couldn't Google someone's name to find them, but, King David had plenty of connections and it wasn't long until someone came to him with information about Mephibosheth. He was now a grown man with a son of his own. All these years he was still living in Lodebar. Remember, it was fear that drove them to this place. Mephibosheth's name means: he who scatters shame or destroys shame. His uncle, Ishobeth's name means: man of shame—he was a younger son of Saul and ruled as king for two years after Saul's death. The name "Lodebar" means: without pasture, barren, dry, nothing can grow and flourish. And the root word means: failed, futile, incapable, unreliable, a nothing, ignorant, cannot, illiterate, unimportant, useless, worthless, and on and on!

Mephibosheth lived under a distorted identity. His grandfather had been a king, his father was a prince, and fear had driven him to a place of total despair, hopelessness, disappointments, and misery. By birth he was royalty, but he was living as a pauper. Although his uncle's name meant man of shame, Mephibosheth had the DNA in him that could destroy shame! This was where Mephibosheth was when David the King (who was a type of Christ) came to him. This was where I was when the King of Kings came to me. Is this your story? If so, the Deliverer has come and His name is Jesus! This story is a picture of Christ and His mercy and grace that has been poured out for us!

At Lodebar, Mephibosheth had probably been fed a daily diet of, "You should have been king, the throne belongs to you, David stole it from you." Lies, lies, and more lies had probably been spoken to him all those years. What lies are holding you captive? Did someone tell you that you were a mistake, that you're no good? Did they tell you they wanted a boy and not a girl, or a girl and not a boy? Those are all lies! Your family may have not planned you, but we know Who did and He has a marvelous plan for your life!

We see from this story how shame and fear kept this man captive for many years, living far beneath his intended destiny. Let's talk about shame for a few minutes.

Shame is not about what you have done, shame is about who you are and that is what is wrong!

Shame always causes us to feel inadequate.

Shame is an identity and dictates who we are.

Shame and rage always interact; where there is rage there is shame.

Shame says I am not good enough, I am less than, I will never measure up.

When a compliment is given to another, it is like an indictment against the person in shame.

Shame eats away at the very foundation of our life.

Shame is a terrible thing under which to live! Guilt says, "I made a mistake!" Shame says, "I am a mistake!" We have difficulty separating *who we are from what we do!*

Mephibosheth knew nothing of the covenant his father and David had made; he was living beneath his covenant rights. When King David came to him, he fell on his face before the presence of the king believing the king had come to kill him. All these years he had lived in poverty, all these years he had lived in fear of what the king would do if he ever found him. Mephibosheth called himself a dead dog. That is what living in Lodebar will do to you. In your mind you are despicable.

Immediately David told him, "Do not fear. For I will surely show you kindness for the sake of your father, Jonathan." And if that wasn't enough, David went on to tell him, "I will restore to you all the land of your grandfather Saul and you shall eat at my table regularly".

The last time we read of Mephibosheth is found in II Samuel 19:24–30. David's son, Abaslom had rebelled against his father and was gathering people to make himself king, rather than David. David was forced to leave Jerusalem. Ziba, Mephibosheth's long time servant, hurried to the aid of David, but Ziba lied to David about Mephibosheth and insinuated Mephobisheth was not being loyal to the king. He did this in order to gain Mephibosheth's estate for his own. (II SAMUEL 16.) David did not question the truthfulness of Ziba and gave the entire estate over to him.

Mephibosheth knew that David's life was in danger and he mourned for the safety of David, this one who had come to him and accepted him just as he was. But Mephobisheth, though he was a cripple, risked his own life by trying to follow David into exile. When he met up with David and explained what had happened, David was unwilling to decide between the two accounts he had heard and compromised by saying that the land would be equally divided. Mephobisheth, now that he had been in the presence of the king and his heart was being changed and transformed said, *"Let Ziba have it all* since my lord, the king, has come safely to his own house."

You see, something happened to Mephobisheth. He came into a place of trust and faith, and knew that worldly riches could be taken away, but what he now had in relationship with the King could never be taken away. Why worry and fret over such a small thing?

This is such a beautiful story of redemption and this could very well be your story Mephibosheth continued to walk with a limp; He did not walk correctly. But that should not keep us from eating at the king's table. Fear drove Mephibosheth from his home and it was fear that caused the original crippling accident—someone dropped him! It was not his fault! But because he believed a lie, that lie kept him captive all those years until the King came and delivered him. What lie or lies are you believing?

As I have already mentioned several times, I came from a very dysfunctional home (this means; abnormal, impaired.) We were impaired in numerous ways, but as I have grown and matured, I see that my parents did the best they knew to do. They were damaged as well. In my early days of growing in the things of God, I would be asked to share my testimony quite often. I want to share something with you that I feel God dropped in my heart and it has been very helpful to me through the years.

"Elaine, it is true, the home you grew up in definitely helped shape the person that you became, but if you continue to use that as an excuse for your own mistakes and failures—as a crutch—then you will always walk as a cripple. But if you are willing to lay down these "crutches" and lean into Me, then I will cause you to walk in wholeness."

As I said, He spoke this to me early on and it has been like a compass to give me direction. We make excuses for the way we are, but with Christ we can change.

Living Expectantly

I love Psalm 51. This psalm was written by David after he had sinned with Bathsheba. Nathan, the prophet came to him and said to him, "David, you are the man!" David took total blame for what had happened. He did not blame Bathsheba, his parents, or anyone else. He took full responsibility for his sin, and thirty-three times in this one psalm David referred to himself as being at fault. He knew his sin was primarily against God! No wonder David was known as a man after the heart of God!

Yes, my parents failed me. I have failed my own children time and time again. But I know deep within my heart that my parents loved me very much and with the knowledge they had at the time they were raising me, they did the very best they knew how. Without making excuses for them, in their day people didn't know a lot about healing, deliverance, etc. My parents had clipped wings and were never able to soar as God intended. Yes, we may be products of our past, but we don't have to remain prisoners of our past. If we were perfect we wouldn't need a Savior, would we? God is a perfect parent, but look at His kids! We all need a Savior and Jesus is His name.

Fear and shame will cripple us, keep us bound. We have a fear of being known as we really are. *If you knew the areas where I am crippled, would you still love me, would you accept me, would you reject me?!?* These are our fears. We are afraid to let anyone know of our past, we're afraid to let anyone know of our struggles, so we continue to be bound and crippled. *We are afraid for you to know that I have been and might still be at Lodebar.* But no longer do you have to walk in fear. The king has invited you to come and eat at His table. Your crippled condition is not seen under the King's table! The invitation has been extended: come and eat! The King found Mephibosheth at Lodebar, that desolate, barren and futile place, but Mephibosheth left there and went to Jerusalem, the city of peace.

Yes, after getting pregnant and putting the child up for adoption, I started wearing a coat of shame. It became my identity. Like Mephibosheth I was living in

> **Yes, we may be products of our past, but we don't have to remain prisoners of our past. If we were perfect we wouldn't need a Savior, would we?**

Lodebar. It was only when I met Jesus the King, and He offered to hide my shame under His table, that I began to walk in the identity that was mine as a new believer. It didn't happen overnight—it has been a process—but as I have learned who I am in Christ, I have taken on His identity and now I have exchanged that coat of shame for the robe of righteousness that Jesus provided for me at the cross.

Perhaps you have gotten in touch with some fear or shame while reading this portion of the book. Let's take a few minutes to pray this prayer and let go of any of these things that might be keeping you in bondage.

"God, You said I am fearfully and wonderfully made. I am not a mistake. You knew all about me even before I came into this world. Today, I choose to let

go of the lies I have been holding on to. I choose to let go of every stronghold I have erected to protect and justify my wrong attitudes, ideas, desires, beliefs, habits, and bad behavior in my life. I renounce these things now and ask for Your forgiveness.

I renounce all agreements I have made with the things I have said about myself and believed about myself that were in direct contradiction to what You have said about me,

(I.e; I am stupid, I am ugly, I will never amount to anything, I was an unwanted child, etc). I renounce all these lies and I choose to embrace Your truth! Teach me Your ways and remove any false ways from me. Today I make a decision to choose life and not death. Thank You Jesus for forgiving me. I receive Your forgiveness and I choose to forgive those that have spoken those negative things over me. I release them from any and all judgments I may have had against them. I give You the coat of shame I have worn as my identity and exchange it for the coat of righteousness that Christ has for me!

"Amen!!"

One More Thing

Have you ever sat in church looking at your watch, your stomach growling, and you're wondering when the preacher is going to stop talking? And then he says, "Let me just say one more thing." And then you know it's not over yet! Please bear with me . . . I am going to end this, I promise, but I do need to say one more thing!

I did not write this book to just make another book, but I have written hoping to make a difference in your life. I wrote hoping to challenge you, the reader, to come up higher in the things of God. God is not looking for great people, but He is looking for people that will prove the greatness of God. I challenge you to learn to expect the unexpected; those things that are beyond anything that you could ask or think. He delights in showing Himself strong on behalf of His children. Jesus always taught expectancy, and expectancy will take us into levels we would never think possible.

Because of Jesus, we have been given one of the greatest privileges. No matter how hopeless things might look or seem, we have hope because of Him. His promises are "Yes" and "Amen." (II CORINTHIANS 1:19) The tragedy today is not unanswered prayer, but prayers never prayed. Find

One More Thing

the promises in His Word and start praying them back to Him. And when you pray BELIEVE you will receive! These are some examples of things you might want to pray:

> Expect your children to serve the Lord.
> Expect light to come into your darkness.
> Expect freedom from your addictions.
> Expect God to turn the tide of the enemy.
> Expect hope when everything seems hopeless.
> Expect God's favor.
> Expect your mourning to be turned into joy.
> Expect God to hear and answer your prayers.
> Expect the backslider to return to their own territory.
> Expect salvation for your household.

"I would have despaired unless I had believed that I would see the goodness of the Lord in the land of the living. Wait for the Lord; be strong and let your heart take courage: Yes, wait for the Lord." PSALM 27:13–14

LIVE EXPECTANTLY!!

Epilogue

Life never seems to be lived in a straight line. There are always curves, detours, and potholes that seem to throw us off, but never just a straight path. Unexpected and often unexplainable things happen that catch us off guard, but God is never surprised. It is in these times when we have to whisper a little prayer and say, "Jesus, I trust You." That is all that is expected of us.

Throughout the book I have shared the wonderful experiences we have had with God. We have been blessed beyond our greatest expectations. At the same time we have been tried beyond what we thought we could bear. We know that every trial has purpose, but at the time you're walking through an ordeal it can be quite difficult. We know grace always supersedes the problem, but knowing this doesn't necessarily lessen the pain. In our trials we are being refined. God is like a Refiner and He allows us to go through the fires in order to remove any impurities (wrong attitudes, motives, issues of the heart, and etc.) His goal is for us to bear His image.

Have you ever heard the story of how fine china is processed? The material that goes into fine china is ground and ground until it is very fine in texture. Then it is positioned in a mold according to the type dish it will be. After that, it is placed in a kiln and the temperature is set at an extremely high degree. An inspector looks over each piece very carefully and grinds away any sharp edges. Once this is completed a glaze is sprayed over the entire surface. To ensure the glaze will adhere to the surface it undergoes a second firing process. An examiner takes the piece out, thumps the object with his finger. If it makes a dull ping then it is returned to the firing process. When the china makes a ping that sounds "musical" then the object is removed from the fire. We want to make sure we keep our attitude right no matter what we are going through and do our best to come forth with a musical sound, right?!?

I want to share with you where we find ourselves at this present time. It was 2009 and though we were in a difficult place trying to care for Bill's 101 year old mother long distance, life was sweet. Bill was a substitute teacher and loved what he was doing. Because he didn't always teach at the same school or have the same students, he still felt, in a small way, he had the opportunity to make a difference in some child's life.

It was a cold winter morning that Bill left the house for an assignment. We were surprised that this particular school was open as many schools had opted to close because of the blizzard like conditions. Bill purposely left earlier than normal in the event he had any problems getting to school. I had just thrown a log on the fire, made myself a cup of tea and was getting ready to have my devotions when the phone rang. It was the school telling me Bill had never arrived.

My granddaughter attended a private school that was also open and my daughter had driven her to school that morning. I called Kayla and asked her to look for her dads' little red pick-up when she started back home.

Mark, our son in law also started searching. He was the one that finally found Bill. Bill traveled on a major freeway, but somehow managed to pull his truck to safety. When Mark reached him he was unconscious. He was taken to the hospital and once they called me I rushed to the hospital. The verdict? A major stroke!

It felt as if our world had suddenly been turned upside down. At times like this there are choices one must make. You can either curse God or bless God, you can either blame God or recognize who the real enemy is, you can either move into hopelessness or choose to hope in the One who never disappoints. You can either trust or doubt, have faith or fear, give up on God or cling to Him as never before. These are just a few of the choices that we must make in order to see God in the most tragic of circumstances.

I have to admit I was scared, hurt, questioning God, disappointed, and so many other emotions I don't recall at present. At the time this seemed harder than when Bill had the brain tumor. I can't explain why, but one thing we were much younger. I do remember at some point crying out to God and saying, "I do not want to drink from this cup!" That was the cry of Jesus as He was facing the cross. (MATTHEW 26:39) For me personally, I wasn't quite sure what that would entail but I felt certain there would be much pain, suffering, and anguish. Yes, Jesus experienced extreme agony from the horrible death of crucifixion but the worst thing as He hung on the cross was the separation from Father God. (MATTHEW 27: 46) Because of Christ in me I would never be separated from Him and I needed to focus on that. I was not alone!

I needed to pour out my heart to the Lord. He was not angry with me. He understood where I was, the things I was feeling, and He hurt with me. He was waiting patiently for me to cast my care on Him as the weight was too cumbersome for me to bear alone. PSALM 62:8 *"Trust in Him at all times, O people; Pour out your heart before Him; God is a refuge for us."* The word pour means to dump or gush. In other words; don't hold back, let it all out. Tell Him exactly what you are feeling. God always responds to those who are real and authentic

Bill's eyes took the brunt of the stroke. Both eyes were closed shut. Of course, we feared he was blind. On the third day one eye opened, not completely, but eventually it finally opened fully. It was thirty days before the other eye opened. While in the hospital they called in a specialist to examine his eyes. When the doctor said, "He is not blind!" I rejoiced. But, with both eyes open he now saw double vision. He wore a patch over one eye for quite awhile, but having to wear glasses over the patch was difficult. We finally decided to cover the lens of his glasses and that has worked. Actually he looks quite debonair with the patch and he gets a lot of attention from children.

We have seen much improvement these past years and I have learned to thank God for the smallest change I see in my husband. It's only been recently that Bill has been able to do some things that he once did before the stroke. I came home one day to see him raking leaves. I can't tell you how happy I was! Of course I bragged and bragged on him and told everyone what he had done. Several days later he decided he would take a little walk. This was a first. I was a little apprehensive about this as his gait is not too steady so I told him I would walk with him. And he responded by saying to me, "If I can rake leaves, I can walk alone!" I have to admit I was nervous. Without him knowing I rushed to the front porch, stood where he could not see me to make sure he would remember where he lived. It reminded me of the days when each one of our children would decide they were big enough to walk to school alone. Thankfully he made it home without any problem and has been taking small walks since that time. I continue to thank God for every step forward that Bill has been able to make. God tells us not to despise the small beginnings. (ZECHARIAH 4:10) We first must learn to thank God for the small things in order to see the bigger things. I still believe our miracle could be right around the corner, so with each step forward I **LIVE EXPECTANTLY!** Mother Teresa once said, "I know God won't give me anything I can't handle. I just wish He didn't trust me so much." If that is true then I'm agreeing with Mother Teresa, I wish He didn't trust us so much!

I John 5:14-15 tells us, "And this is the confidence which we have before Him, that, if we ask anything according to His will, He hears us. And if we know that He hears us in whatever we ask, we know that we have the requests which we have asked from Him." And how do we know His will By studying His word!

Some people have passed on without seeing the promises fulfilled, but God is faithful. Hold on and don't give up! Anthony Flew grew up in a very godly, Christian home. His father was a pastor. They had lived

Epilogue

the life before their son and taught him what the scriptures said. About the age of 15, Anthony, who was very intelligent decided he no longer believed that there was a God and he became a well-known atheist. He published many writings and works on atheism. It was said that he was a foremost evangelist for atheism. His parents were probably broken hearted to see their son deny the teachings he had learned from them, but they continued to pray for him and believed that he would return to the Lord. After their death Anthony did return and wrote an amazing book called, "There is a God: How the World's Most Notorious Atheist Changed His Mind." I would imagine that even though they are in heaven now, they know their son will one day join them. Don't give up. Hold on! It's always too soon to quit!

By the time this book gets in your hands, Bill and I will have celebrated 60 years of marriage. Remember, ours was the marriage that everyone thought would end in divorce. We have certainly had our trials, struggles, and ups and downs. But we have also had blessings upon blessings. We are thankful that God invaded our hearts and made the difference that only He can make in a person's life. Kelly and Kimberly recently celebrated 35 years of marriage. Kayla and Mark celebrated 34 years of marriage and Kyle and Sara have now been married 14 years. Occasionally I ponder the thought of how our family might have ended up had God not come into our home. May we never lose the wonder of who He is and what He is able to do.

Living Expectantly

When I think of all the years we have been married I question how someone can be so young, yet married so long. Yes, we are getting up in years, but still young in heart. Not only has God restored our family . . . He has filled our life with good things, and our youth has been renewed like the eagle's! (PSALM 103:5)